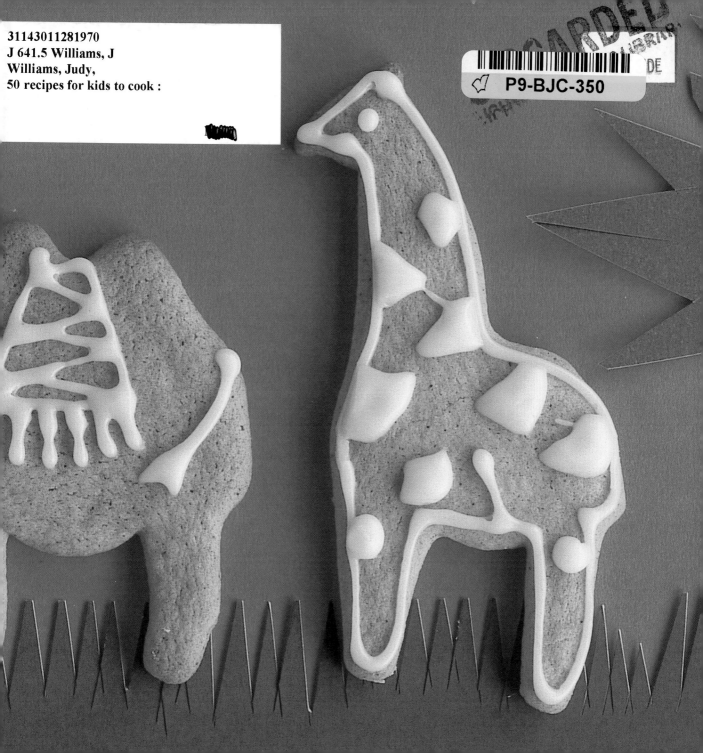

50 RECIPES FOR KIDS TO COOK

50 RECIPES FOR KIDS TO COOK

Tasty food to make yourself shown in step-by-step pictures

Judy Williams

ARMADILLO

This edition is published by Armadillo, an imprint of Anness Publishing Ltd, 108 Great Russell Street, London WC1B 3NA; info@anness.com

www.annesspublishing.com

If you like the images in this book and would like to investigate using them for publishing, promotions or advertising, please visit our website www.practicalpictures.com for more information.

Publisher: Joanna Lorenz
Designers: Lilian Lindblom and Lucy Doncaster
Food and props styling for photography: Judy Williams
Assistant Home Economist: Manisha Kanani
Production controller: Wendy Lawson

PUBLISHER'S NOTE
Although the advice and information in this book are believed to be accurate and true at the time of going to press, neither the authors nor the publisher can accept any legal responsibility or liability for any errors or omissions that may have been made nor for any inaccuracies nor for any loss, harm or injury that comes about from following instructions or advice in this book.

Manufacturer: Anness Publishing Ltd, 108 Great Russell Street, London WC1B 3NA, England
For Product Tracking go to: www.annesspublishing.com/tracking
Batch: 7258-23064-1127

NOTES
Bracketed terms are intended for American readers.
For all recipes, quantities are given in both metric and imperial measures and, where appropriate, in standard cups and spoons. Follow one set of measures, but not a mixture, because they are not interchangeable.
Standard spoon and cup measures are level. 1 tsp = 5ml, 1 tbsp = 15ml, 1 cup = 250ml/8fl oz.
Australian standard tablespoons are 20ml. Australian readers should use 3 tsp in place of 1 tbsp for measuring small quantities.
American pints are 16fl oz/2 cups. American readers should use 20fl oz/2.5 cups in place of 1 pint when measuring liquids.
Electric oven temperatures in this book are for conventional ovens. When using a fan oven, the temperature will probably need to be reduced by about 10-20°C/20-40°F. Since ovens vary, you should check with your manufacturer's instruction book for guidance. Medium (US large) eggs are used unless otherwise stated.

CONTENTS

Introduction

Welcome to the wonderful world of food. We all need it, we all eat it and now you're going to find out how to cook it.

It would be easy never to prepare a meal again – supermarkets are choc-a-bloc with ready-made meals, but where's the fun in that? It's true you'll have to find time to shop and get everything ready, as well as doing the actual cooking, but the thrill of serving and eating something you have made with your own clean hands is fantastic.

This book is split into sections. The first part is the bossy bit, which tells you what to do and what not to do to be safe in the kitchen. Then there's lots of information about equipment and about words used in cooking that you might not understand. After that it's on to the exciting part – choosing what to cook. Some recipes are simple and these are a good place to start, if you haven't done any cooking before. There are also lots of recipes that seem more difficult but, in fact, just take a bit longer.

All basic cooking techniques have been included in one recipe or another, so you will learn lots of useful skills that can be swapped around as you get more experienced. These skills may be useful for some school exams, and will certainly be invaluable when you leave home and have to feed yourself. You'll probably be feeding your friends as well, once they learn of your talents!

As well as stacks of snacks and main meals, there are plenty of desserts, cakes and cookies to choose from, with chocolate included in as many as possible!

So get cooking and have a great time!

Safety First

The kitchen is full of things that could be very dangerous, such as electrical sockets, hot ovens and hobs, fast-moving equipment and hot pans and baking pans. It's therefore very important that you take as much care as possible.

Use a kitchen stool to raise you up to the level of the work surface.

• Tie long hair back while you are cooking – then it can't get caught on equipment, will be kept away from flames and won't become an extra ingredient in your recipe!

• Always wash your hands – not just when you begin to cook, but as you handle different ingredients. Garlic-tainted cakes are horrible and no one finds grey pastry nice!

• Water and electricity do not mix, so dry your hands well before touching any sockets or plugging in machinery, and **an adult should always supervise**. Switch off before pulling out the plug.

• Read through the recipe before you start. Have everything ready: panic causes problems!

• Protect your clothes: wear an apron or old shirt if you're a messy cook, and roll up those sleeves!

• Washing-up is the most boring part about cooking, so keep it to a minimum and wash up as much as possible as you go along. Or stack the dishwasher, of course, but in all events, try to leave the room tidy or your days in the kitchen may be numbered!

• Is the work surface too high? Making pastry or cakes means working in a mixing bowl and it might be hard to get your hands right in there. Put the bowl on the kitchen table or stand it in the empty sink instead, as both these places are lower than a work surface. Or use a kitchen stool.

• Too hot to handle? Always use oven gloves (mitts) or a thickly folded, dry dish towel (wet ones let the heat straight through) when handling hot things and always **ask an adult** to lift things in and out of the oven. Keep pan handles turned away from any heat source and check they aren't hot, before trying to lift the pan.

• Some recipes call for hot liquids and foods to be drained or poured into something else. Please do this very carefully, always **with adult supervision**, or **ask an adult** to do it for you.

• Do not overfill the pan and, if it is too heavy or you aren't sure you can manage, ask a grown-up for some help.

• A helping hand? Watch out for younger members of the family who want to help, especially if the oven is hot or you are frying things. If they really will not go away, find them something simple to do, such as arranging tomatoes in a bowl, or greasing cake tins (pans). Alternatively, give them a small piece of pastry or dough to play with. Pets can also be a hazard: they creep in and try to trip you up, so bear them in mind.

• Whoops-a-daisy: any wet spills on the floor, especially oil, should be wiped up immediately. Use hot, soapy water and then rub the area dry so the floor does not become a skating rink.

None of this is really complicated: it is a matter of being careful and sensible, and thinking about what you are doing. Remember that most accidents happen in the home: make sure your home is not the site of of them!

Wash your hands before cooking.

Tie up long hair.

Getting Switched On

Although some dishes do not need cooking, the majority in this book do, so you need to know how to use ovens, hobs and microwaves correctly and safely.

Cookers

There are lots of different types of oven but you are sure to have one of the more popular ones. They are made to work using different sorts of energy and each one has its own temperature guide, which explains why recipes have a choice of three settings for preheating the oven, for example, 'Cook at 200°C/400°F/Gas 6'. If you have an electric cooker that works at Centigrade temperature (°C), use the first number, for an electric cooker that uses Fahrenheit (°F), use the second number, and for a gas cooker use the last number.

The oven is hottest on the top shelf, although most things are best cooked on the middle one. If two baking trays are going in at the same time, the one nearer the top of the oven will be cooked more quickly. You can switch the trays round halfway through.

Take great care when using a hob.

When the recipe says to preheat the oven, remember it will take about 10 minutes to reach the specified temperature; if you put the food in before the oven is hot enough, it will take longer to cook and some food, such as cakes, will not cook correctly.

Cookers usually have three different cooking places – the oven, the grill (broiler) and the hob.
• The oven cooks large items of food slowly and evenly, with the minimum of attention.
• The grill cooks quickly, so grilled (broiled) food must be smaller and thinner or the outside will burn before the middle is properly cooked (even though there is a temperature control). You have to keep a close watch on the food and it will need to be turned often.

Safety First for Ovens and Hobs

When the oven is working, the door becomes very hot and this can be dangerous if you have younger brothers and sisters who want to help. If your cooker is new it may have a stay-cool door, which is much safer. Otherwise, watch out for this or ask your parents to fit a special safety screen to the front of the oven.

You should always have **adult supervision** whenever you use the oven or hob, and it is often best if they lift things in and out of the oven for you to avoid any chance of an accident.

Ask an adult to take things in and out of the oven, wearing oven gloves.

• The hob is the name for the burners or hot plates on the top of the oven: in some kitchens, the hob is separate from the oven. You use pans or frying pans to cook food on the hob. Control-knobs can be turned up to cook things more quickly, or turned down low to cook more slowly.

Microwave Ovens

These machines make all the water molecules in food jump around and heat up, which cooks food quickly. They are brilliant at thawing frozen food, re-heating cooked food, melting chocolate

Safety First for Microwave Ovens

Never put any foil, metal dishes or plates with metallic edges in microwaves, and follow recipe instructions carefully.

The standing time mentioned at the end of lots of microwave recipes is part of the cooking, so don't be tempted to skip it.

and cooking baked potatoes, and you can make some cakes and desserts in them too. They cannot usually turn food brown.

Timers

Modern cookers often have a built-in timer, rather like an alarm clock. Set it to the recommended cooking time and it makes a buzzing noise that reminds you to take the food out. Microwaves also have a timer, and usually beep and stop cooking when the time is up.

Green Tips for Ovens and Hobs

Save energy and cut fuel bills:
• Only use as much water as you need in pans and kettles.
• Put lids on pans and reduce the heat once the contents have come to the boil.
• Flames that lick up the sides of a pan are wasting energy, so adjust the flame.
• Steam a second vegetable in a colander over the potatoes.
• Try to cook more than one thing in the oven at a time.

Working Tools

There are probably lots of weird and wonderful things in the kitchen cupboards and drawers, so here is a handy guide to help you find out what they do.

Food Processor

This is actually a giant blender, with a large bowl and, usually, lots of attachments. The metal chopping blade is the one we use most; it's best with dry ingredients like vegetables and pastry. The plastic blade is for batters and cakes. Some processors also have grating blades and slicing plates. **An adult must always supervise** when you use a food processor and great care must be taken when handling the sharp blades.

Electric Whisk

A whisk's main function is to beat in air and make the mixture bigger and thicker, as in, for example, cream and cake mixtures. But a whisk can also blend things, such as sauces, together and make them smooth.

Blenders

Also called liquidizers, these are usually attached to an electric whisk motor or a food processor and are tall and deep, with blades at the base. Ideal for turning things into liquid such as fruit for sauces, soups and milk shakes. Hand-held blenders are much smaller and can be used in a small bowl or mug.

If you are blending soups, always makes sure the mixture has cooled down before you blend it, just in case it splatters a bit. You can also place a clean dish towel over the top of the blender to catch and splashes. You also need to make sure you have fitted the lid securely!

Chopping Boards

Lots of people use the same board for all their preparation, but it is much more hygenic to use a different one for each type of job. It is possible to buy boards in different shades, so the same one is always used for the same job. A wooden board is best for cutting bread. Scrub boards well after use.

Graters

A pyramid-shaped or box-shaped grater is the most useful type. Each side has a different grating surface, made up of small, curved, raised blades. Use the coarsest one for vegetables and cheese, and the finer sides for grating orange and lemon rind. Stand the grater on a flat surface while you use it, and grated food collects inside the pyramid. Scrub well with a brush after use. There are also very small graters, for whole nutmegs.

Measuring Equipment

Most homes have some sort of measuring equipment, whether this is scales, spoons or cups.

> ### Safety First for Whisks, Blenders and Processors
> Never put your hand in the processor to move something while it is plugged in. And keep small fingers away from whisks while they are whizzing round. Treat all electrical equipment very carefully and unplug everything before you fiddle around with blades.

Recipes seem to have lots of weights listed, and this is because different countries use different ways to measure things. As long as you stick to the same ones for each recipe, you should not have any problems.

The metric quantity is mentioned first, such as 115g, followed by the imperial measurement – 4oz – and then the American cup measurement. These are ways to measure dry ingredients, such as flour, sugar and chocolate.

When you measure liquids, there are three measurements to choose from. The metric measurement, such as 300ml, followed by the imperial one – $\frac{1}{2}$ pint – and, finally, the American cup measure – $1\frac{1}{4}$ cups. Most measuring jugs (cups) have all of these measurements written on the side for easy measuring.

Small amounts of both dry and wet ingredients are often measured in millilitres (ml) and tablespoons (tbsp). 15ml is the same as 1 tbsp and 5ml is the same as 1 teaspoon (1 tsp). The spoon should be level, and it is worth using proper measuring spoons rather than ones from the cutlery drawer.

Bowls

Mixing bowls come in all sorts of sizes and the most useful are made from heatproof glass. Use large ones for pastry, bread-making and whisking egg whites; smaller ones are better for smaller quantities, such as beating eggs and mixing dips.

Pans

Different types of pans and frying pans can be made from different metals. They need to have a thick base to stop food from sticking. They usually have lids, which prevent food drying out if it is cooking for a long time.

colander

nutmeg grater

baking tray

bun tin

pan

springform
cake tins

pans

frying pan

measuring
cups

box
grater

weighing scales

whisks

food processor

hand-held whisk

mixing bowls

stick blender

chopping boards

measuring spoons

measuring jug

Small Tools

In addition to large equipment, loads of small tools are extremely useful in the kitchen for preparing food for cooking. This is just a small selection.

Can opener
The two 'arms' are squeezed together, so the blades at the top pierce the can. Turn the handle round and round and the top of the can will come off.

Canelle knife
This is rather like a zester, but cuts a thicker strip of rind.

Corer
Looks rather like a potato peeler but has a tube of metal that is pushed through the centre of an apple to pull out the core.

Fish slice
For lifting and turning burgers, fish, or even eggs!

Garlic press
Squashes the garlic cloves through small holes ready for cooking; you need a brush with stiff bristles to poke through the holes to get it clean again.

Hand whisk
A spring whisk is most effective, especially for cream or eggs.

Kitchen scissors
Used for cutting things like bacon, but also perfect for snipping herbs.

Knives
Knives must be used very carefully, and always **with adult supervision**. Don't use a huge bread knife to peel an apple: pick the right size for the right job and try not to be distracted. No conducting with the carving knife!

All knives get blunt after a while and should be sharpened carefully, **by an adult**, using a special knife-sharpening gadget.
You will only need five basic knives to do most jobs in this book.
• *Paring knife*, with an 8cm/3in blade, for peeling and trimming fruit and vegetables.
• *Cook's knife*, with a 15cm/6in blade, for general slicing.
• *Chopping knife*, with a 20cm/8in blade, for chopping and slicing.
• *Bread knife*, with a 25cm/10in serrated-edge blade, for cutting bread, and removing the skin from a pineapple!
• *Palette knife (spatula),* with a long, flexible blade, for lifting and spreading.

Ladle
A large, deep spoon, used mainly for serving soup.

Lemon squeezer
The cut side of a halved citrus fruit is pressed down and squeezed over the central 'spike'. The juice runs down and collects, ready for pouring.

Pastry brush
For brushing egg on to pastry; also good for brushing sauces or oil over meat or vegetables.

Pastry wheel
Used for making a decoratively cut edge for pastry or ravioli.

Piping bag and nozzles
Big ones are best for cookie mixes. A nozzle is dropped into the bag until it peeps out of the other end. Small ones are better for piping icing.

Potato peeler
Some have fixed peeler blades with wooden handles; other have a more mobile blade and this can make peeling easier.

Rolling pin
Usually wooden, although marble ones keep pastry cool.

Rubber spatula
A wooden handle with a flexible blade, it's very good at getting mixing bowls clean.

Sieves (strainers)
These come in various sizes. A small one is ideal for sifting icing (confectioners') sugar over cakes. Larger ones are used for sifting flour and draining vegetables.

Skewers
Metal or wooden ones are used for kebabs; metal ones are also good for pushing into cakes, to see if they're cooked.

Slotted spoon
For lifting and draining food.

Tongs
Used for turning things over.

Wooden spoons
Come in various lengths. Short ones are better for beating cake mixtures and chocolate, but ones with longer handles are better for cooking on the hob, because your hand is further from the heat.

Zester
A small tool with five tiny round blades at the end. When it is dragged across an orange or lemon, it removes long thin shreds of rind.

lemon squeezer

fish slice

hand whisk

piping bag and nozzles

slotted spoon

ladle

sieves

tongs

potato peelers

canelle knife

zester

apple corer

potato masher

rolling pin

can opener

rubber spatula

garlic press

wooden spoon

pastry brush

pastry wheel

scissors

palette knife

skewers

knives

A–Z of Cooking Terms

Sometimes cooking seems like a foreign language, with lots of words you are not sure about. Hopefully this A–Z guide will explain what most of them mean, and then you will be off your marks and in action in the kitchen.

Folding chocolate into cream.

Grating cheese.

Bake
To cook in the oven, in dry heat, at a set temperature.

Barbecue
A method of cooking food over glowing charcoal, which gives food a smoky taste.

Baste
To spoon fat and cooking juices over meat whilst cooking, to keep the meat tender and moist.

Blend
To mix ingredients evenly. Also used to describe the action of a blender.

Boil
A liquid is boiling when the edges are rolling over and large bubbles are heaving in the surface. This is called a rolling boil and that is how it looks. Usually, at this point, the heat is turned down and the liquid starts to simmer. There are not many things that are cooked at a rolling boil, except raw beans, pasta and caramel. The action would be too fierce for most vegetables.

Bone
To remove bones from meat, fish or poultry.

Brown
Meat and vegetables are often browned to give a more intense taste. The food is turned over frequently, usually in hot fat.

Core
To cut out the tough central part and seeds of a fruit. This is easiest done with a corer. Push it into the apple, over the stalk, and twist. Pull the corer and the core out.

Cream
To beat fat (usually butter or magarine) and sugar together until they are light and fluffy when making cakes.

Dredge
To cover something with an even layer of flour or sugar, dredging chocolate brownies with icing (confectioners') sugar for instance.

Dust
To sprinkle food lightly with flour or sugar – like dusting a loaf with flour before baking.

Flake
To divide cooked fish into its natural flakes having removed any skin and bones.

Fold in
To add something to a mixture very gently, so as not to break up all the air bubbles – as when folding whisked egg white into soufflés, and flour into sponge cakes – so the mixture stays light and fluffy.

Fry
To cook food in hot fat or oil, usually to get a crisp, browned surface on the outside.

Garnish
To decorate food with herbs, chopped vegetables or fruit, to make it look attractive for serving.

Glaze
Brushing pastry or bread with egg or milk, which will make it shiny and look more attractive. It will also seal a pastry case and prevent the filling running out.

Grate
To shred into tiny strips using a grater. (See also page 18).

Grease
Brushing cooking tins (pans) or trays with a little oil or a butter wrapper helps to prevent food from sticking while it cooks.

Knead
To work dough until it is smooth and elastic (stretchy).

Line a tin (pan)
Putting a paper lining inside the tin, to prevent food sticking.

Marinade
An infused liquid, usually non-sweet and using oil, lemon juice or wine. Meat is sometimes soaked in a marinade to make it more tender and tasty.

Marinate
To leave meat, fish or poultry in a marinade for a while.

Par-boil
To start cooking food, like potatoes, in boiling water, before moving on to the next stage of the cooking process, such as roasting. Par-boiling speeds up the roasting time.

Peel
To remove the skin from fruit and vegetables, usually using a peeler.

Pipe
To force food from a piping bag through a plain or star nozzle into decorative shapes. Large nozzles might be used for cookies, cream or mashed potato, and smaller ones for icing.

Poach
To cook food gently in simmering, not boiling, water.

Prove
Once bread dough has been kneaded for 5 minutes and is smooth and elastic, it is covered with a clean dish towel and left somewhere warm to double in size. This process is called proving the dough.

Peeling an apple.

Rubbing fat into flour.

Separating an egg.

Weighing dry ingredients.

Purée
To turn soft, solid food into a smoother thicker food – for example, lumpy vegetable soup can be puréed in a blender to make it smooth.

Roast
To cook uncovered in the oven by dry heat. Meat, chicken and vegetables are often roasted, but you can also roast nuts and seeds.

Roux
Equal quantities of butter and flour are cooked together, to make the thickening for a white sauce. The fat will be melted in a pan and then the flour mixed in. A roux should be cooked gently for 1–2 minutes before the liquid, usually milk, is added and whisked constantly over a low heat to make a thick sauce.

Rub in
To mix the fat into the flour when making pastry, crumble topping and some cakes. Use your fingertips to lift lumps of fat and flour and rub them together to break the fat into smaller and smaller pieces, until it looks like breadcrumbs. Hold your fingers high over the bowl to mix air into the mixture at the same time.

Seasoning
This term usually means to add salt and pepper to dishes, to heighten the taste. Other aromatic ingredients added in small quantities, such as herbs or some spices, could also be called seasonings.

Separating an egg
Some recipes require only the white or the yolk of an egg, so you need to be able to separate them. This technique is shown on page 18.

Shallow-fry
To cook food in a thin layer of oil, so it browns and crisps on the outside. You usually need to flip the food halfway through cooking, using a spatula.

Sift
To shake dry foods through a sieve or strainer to remove any lumps. Also used to purée foods by pushing through the strainer, as an alternative to using a blender or food processor.

Simmer
To reduce the heat once the liquid has come to the boil so the liquid still bubbles lightly and is not completely calm.

Snipping
Using kitchen scissors to cut things in small pieces, rather than chopping them. This is a good way to cut up bacon, herbs, dried fruits and bread.

Stir-fry
A fast way to cook food over a high heat in very little oil. Food must be cut into small even-sized pieces and kept moving all the time to stop it burning. This is traditionally done in a wok, but a frying pan can be used instead.

Stock
A tasty liquid that is used to make soups and cook rice. Vegetable trimmings and bones can be boiled in water and the water turns to stock as it picks up the taste. It is quicker and easier to use stock (bouillon) cubes. They come in lots of types, so choose the one that suits your recipe best, for example, use chicken stock cubes for chicken dishes. Usually one stock cube is enough to make 600ml/1 pint/ 2½ cups of stock, but check the packet instructions.

Thicken
To give thinner sauces and gravies more body, by adding a thickening agent, such as cornflour (cornstarch). Mix it with a little water and pour it into the boiling liquid, stirring all the time (to stop it going lumpy), until it comes back to the boil and the liquid starts to thicken.

Weighing
It is very important that you weigh out ingredients carefully, especially when baking as even the tiniest bit too much or too little can have a big effect on the finished food. You can get scales with a circular dial or digital ones, which tend to be a bit more accurate and easier to use.

Whisk
To mix air into egg whites or yolks. Whisked egg whites go through several different stages as they thicken, so check the recipe carefully. 'Soft peaks' means the egg white will stand in peaks but the tops will flop over. 'Stiff peaks' means the peaks will not flop over; finally they become stiff and look dry.

Zest
To remove the coloured part of the rind of citrus fruit (lemons, oranges, etc.) Use a fine grater or a zester (see page 18).

Preparing Onions

Many recipes require chopped onions. Making the onions a similar size means they all cook at the same time, but we don't want any sliced fingertips, so take care!

1 With adult supervision, cut the onion in half with the skin still on. Lie the cut side flat on a board. Trim off both ends. Peel off the skin.

2 Make several parallel cuts lengthways (from trimmed end to end), but not cutting right to one end, so it remains intact.

3 Make cuts at right angles to the first ones, at the same distance apart. The onion will be finely chopped. Finally, chop the end that was in one piece.

COOK'S TIP
When an onion is described as 'sliced', cut down through each half to make vertical half-moon slices.

Preparing Carrots

Although they are often just sliced in circles as these cook most quickly, carrots can look much more attractive when they are cut in a different way.

1 Peel the carrot, using this quick method with a swivel peeler, and trim the ends with a sharp knife, **with adult supervision**.

2 Cut the carrot into short lengths and then into thin slices, lengthways. You will need a sharp knife for this job, so be careful.

3 Cut each thin slice into fine strips, about the size of matchsticks.

COOK'S TIP
Use tiny cutters to stamp out shapes from the thin carrot slices, to garnish soups or salads.

Grating Fresh Root Ginger

Ground ginger powder is fine in cakes, but when it comes to a stir-fry, it has to be fresh.

1 The size is often given as a measurement, because the root is long and knobbly and difficult to weigh accurately. Break off roughly the quantity you need.

2 **With adult supervision**, use a peeler, or sharp knife if the ginger is really lumpy, and cut away the tough outer layer.

3 Grate on the coarsest side of the grater and use the strips for your recipe. Don't use any hard or stringy bits of ginger.

COOK'S TIP
Fresh root ginger has a strong, spicy, taste, so don't put in too much if you don't like hot food.

Grating Lemon Rind and Squeezing Lemon Juice

Recipes sometimes call for the grated rind and juice of a lemon to add a bright, fragrant taste to dishes.

1 Rinse the lemon, unless it was marked 'unwaxed'. Rub the lemon up and down the fine grating side of the grater, until the yellow rind has come off. Stop grating once the white pith underneath shows through. Keep moving the lemon round the grater, until all the yellow rind is off.

2 Cut the lemon in half, press one half down on to the pointed part of the squeezer and twist. Keep pressing and twisting and the juice will come out of the lemon. The larger pips all collect at the base and are held back by the glass or plastic 'teeth'.

3 Smaller pips might sneak through. Either fish them out with a spoon or your fingers, or pour the juice through a small strainer, before adding it to the mixture.

COOK'S TIP
Oranges and limes may be grated and squeezed the same way.

Separating Eggs

Meringues and some sauces call for just egg whites, so they must be separated from the yolk.

1 Break the egg on to a saucer carefully, taking care not to break the yolk.

2 Stand an egg cup over the yolk and hold it firmly in place, taking care not to puncture the yolk.

3 Hold the saucer over the mixing bowl and let the egg white slide in, hanging on to the egg cup. The yolk will be left on the saucer.

COOK'S TIP
The yolk can be used for glazing pastry or in lots of other recipes, so don't just throw it away.

Grating

The most popular grater is the pyramid or box type, which offers different-sized blades for grating.

1 The very fine side is for grating whole nutmeg. Hold the nutmeg in one hand and rub it up and down the grater. Sometimes, it is easier to do this directly over the food.

2 The finer blades are best for citrus fruits. The blades only work downwards and you might need to brush out some of the rind from the inside with a dry pastry brush.

3 The coarsest side is best for cheese, fruit and vegetables. The blades work when you press downwards and the food will collect inside the grater.

COOK'S TIP
The jagged punched holes down one side of the grater are ideal for making breadcrumbs.

Whipping Cream

Cream can be bought in various thicknesses, so choose double (heavy) or whipping cream, if you need it to be thick for your recipe. Do not try whipping single (light) cream!

1 Pour the cream into a bowl and use an electric mixer to whip the cream. Keep the electric mixer moving around as you whisk.

2 A hand-held whisk also works well but it takes much longer and makes your arm tired! The cream will first reach a soft and floppy stage, then get thicker and thicker the more you whisk.

3 Once whisk lines are left in the cream and it looks fairly stiff, it's time to stop whipping. Cream will start to look like mashed potato as it curdles and reaches the over-whipped stage.

Lining a Tin

Stop food, mainly cakes, sticking to the cooking tin (pan) by lining the tin with baking parchment.

1 Stand the tin on the paper and draw round the base. Cut out the shape, just inside the line.

2 Wrap a strip of paper round the outside of the tin and cut it 5cm/2in longer and 5cm/1/2in wider.

3 Fold one long edge over by 2.5cm/1in. Make diagonal cuts at regular intervals up to the fold. Grease the tin lightly, to help the paper stick to it. Put the long strip inside the tin, round the edges, so the fringed paper sits on the base. Lie the round piece of paper over the top.

COOK'S TIP
If you only need to base-line a tin, and not line the sides as well, just follow step 1.

Making Mashed Potatoes

Check the label on the bags to see which potatoes are good for mashing, or ask your greengrocer.

SERVES 4
450g/1lb potatoes, peeled and
  quartered
25g/1oz/2 tbsp butter
30ml/2 tbsp milk or cream
salt and pepper

COOK'S TIP
Add two crushed cloves of garlic or a handful of chopped fresh herbs, to make a real change.

1 Put the potatoes in a pan with enough room to mash them. Cover with water, add a little salt and bring the water to the boil. Turn down the heat and simmer for 20–25 minutes. The potatoes should feel tender and fall off a sharp knife when cooked.

2 With adult supervision, drain the potatoes in a colander and return them to the pan. Add the butter, milk or cream and black pepper and use a potato masher to squash the potatoes and flatten all the lumps. Add more milk if you like them really soft.

Cooking Rice

Measure rice in a jug or cup, by volume rather than by weight, for best results.

SERVES 2
10ml/2 tsp oil
150ml/¼ pint/⅔ cup long grain
  white rice
300ml/½ pint/1¼ cups boiling
  water or stock
salt

COOK'S TIP
Some types of easy-cook (converted) rice may not take as long as standard rice; check cooking times on the packet.

1 Heat the oil in a pan and add the rice. Stir to coat all the grains with the oil.

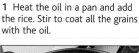

2 With adult supervision, pour on the boiling water or stock, add a little salt and stir once, before putting on the lid. Turn down the heat so the liquid is just simmering gently. Leave it alone for 15 minutes.

3 Lift the lid carefully (away from you) and check whether the rice is tender and that the liquid has almost gone. Fluff up the grains of rice with a fork to separate them and serve immediately.

Cooking Pasta

Pasta comes in loads of different shapes, sizes and shades. Green pasta has spinach in it, red pasta has tomato and brown pasta is made from whole-wheat flour. Egg pasta has extra eggs in the dough. Allow about 115g/4oz dried pasta per person if it is the main ingredient, and a little less if it is to accompany a meal, although this may vary according to how hungry you are!

SERVES 4
350–450 g/12oz–1lb dried
   pasta
salt

COOK'S TIP
Fresh pasta is also available, but its cooking times are shorter – check the packet instructions.

2 Cook for 8–12 minutes, depending on what type of pasta you are using – spaghetti will not take as long as the thicker penne pasta. It should be al dente when cooked, which means it still has some firmness to it and isn't completely soft and soggy.

1 Bring a large pan of water to the boil. Add a little salt. **With adult supervision**, add the pasta to the pan, a little at a time, so that the water stays at a rolling boil.

3 **With adult supervision**, drain the pasta well in a colander and tip it back to the pan. Pour a sauce over or toss in a little melted butter.

Making a Salad Dressing

Green or mixed salads add crunch and freshness to heavy, meaty meals such as lasagne or barbecued ribs, but they are bland and boring without a dressing like this one.

SERVES 4
15ml/1 tbsp white wine vinegar
10ml/2 tsp coarse-grain
   mustard
salt
freshly ground black pepper
30ml/2 tbsp oil

COOK'S TIP
Mix 30ml/2 tbsp oil with 15ml/ 1 tbsp lemon juice, for a tangier dressing. Add chopped fresh herbs for extra taste.

1 Put the vinegar and mustard in a bowl or jug (pitcher). Whisk well, then add a little salt and pepper.

2 Add the oil slowly, about 5ml/1 tsp at a time, whisking constantly. Pour the dressing over the salad just before serving so that the lettuce stays crisp. Use two spoons to toss the salad and coat it with the dressing.

Skinny Dips

Jacket potatoes in disguise, with a delicious spicy dip.

SERVES 4
8 large potatoes, scrubbed
30–45ml/2–3 tbsp oil
90ml/6 tbsp mayonnaise
30ml/2 tbsp natural
   (plain) yogurt
5ml/1 tsp curry paste
30ml/2 tbsp roughly chopped
   fresh coriander (cilantro)
salt

COOK'S TIP
If there is just one of you, prick
one large potato all over with a
fork and microwave on HIGH for
6–8 minutes, until tender. Scoop
out the middle, brush with oil and
grill (broil) until browned.

VARIATION
You can use really mild curry paste
if you don't like spicy food, or
replace it with 5ml/1 tsp tomato
purée (paste).

1 Preheat the oven to 190°C/375°F/
Gas 5. Arrange the potatoes in a
roasting pan, prick them all over
with a fork and cook for 45 minutes,
or until tender. Leave to cool slightly.

2 With adult supervision, cut
each potato into quarters
lengthways, holding the potato
firmly in place with a clean dish
towel if it's still a bit hot.

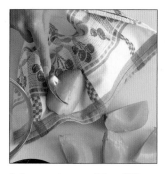

3 Scoop out some of the middle
with a knife or spoon and put the
skins back in the roasting pan.
Save the cooked potato for making
fish cakes.

4 Brush the skins with oil and
sprinkle with salt before **asking an
adult** to put them back in the oven.
Cook for 30–40 minutes more, until
they are crisp and brown, brushing
them occasionally with more oil.

5 Meanwhile, put the mayonnaise,
yogurt, curry paste and 15ml/1 tbsp
chopped coriander in a small bowl
and mix together well. Leave for
30–40 minutes to allow the taste
to develop.

6 Put the dip in a clean bowl and
arrange the skins around the edge.
Serve hot, sprinkled with the
remaining fresh coriander.

Veggie Stir-fry

Ideal for those vegetarians out there, this speedy snack is good on its own, or on toast or with crusty bread. If you're really starving, add a few prawn crackers.

SERVES 4
2 garlic cloves
4 large flat mushrooms
4 spring onions (scallions)
1 carrot
6 baby corn
75g/3oz fine green beans
50g/2oz/¼ cup butter
2.5cm/1in piece fresh root
 ginger, grated
30ml/2 tbsp soy sauce
115g/4oz beansprouts, rinsed
 and drained

COOK'S TIP
Do not be tempted to wash mushrooms, as this will ruin them and make them very soggy. Instead brush off any dry dirt and then wipe them with a damp piece of kitchen paper or, if they are really still dirty, carefully peel off the outer skin using a small sharp knife, **with adult supervision**.

1 With adult supervision, peel and crush the garlic cloves, wipe clean the mushrooms and cut the spring onions into 2.5cm/1in pieces. Cut the carrot into matchsticks, quarter the baby corn lengthways and cut the fine green beans in half.

2 With adult supervision, melt the butter in a large frying pan and fry the garlic until it has softened. Put the mushrooms in the pan and fry gently for 8–10 minutes, turning once or twice, until tender. Lift out the mushrooms, place in a dish and cover to keep them hot.

3 Turn up the heat and add the ginger, spring onions, carrot, corn and beans to the frying pan and stir-fry for 2 minutes, keeping everything moving.

4 Add the soy sauce and beansprouts and cook for 1 minute more. Put each mushroom on a plate and top with the stir-fried vegetables. Serve immediately.

Nutty Chicken Kebabs

A tasty Thai appetizer that is quick to make and is a real crowd-pleaser. It uses crunchy peanut butter in the dip, making it especially popular with nut-lovers.

SERVES 4
30ml/2 tbsp oil
15ml/1 tbsp lemon juice
450g/1lb skinless chicken breast
  fillets, cut in small cubes

For the dip:
5ml/1 tsp chilli powder
75ml/5 tbsp water
15ml/1 tbsp oil
1 small onion, grated
1 garlic clove, peeled
  and crushed
30ml/2 tbsp lemon juice
60ml/4 tbsp crunchy
  peanut butter
5ml/1 tsp salt
5ml/1 tsp ground coriander
sliced cucumber and lemon
  wedges, to serve

COOK'S TIP
You can use metal skewers instead of wooden ones if you prefer – metal ones won't need soaking as they won't scorch when they are placed under a grill (broiler). Take care when handling them.

1 Soak 12 wooden skewers in water, to prevent them from burning during grilling (broiling). Mix the oil and lemon juice together in a bowl and stir in the cubed chicken. Cover and leave to marinate for at least 30 minutes.

2 Thread four or five cubes on each wooden skewer. **With adult supervision**, cook under a hot grill (broiler), turning often, until cooked and browned. This will take about 10 minutes. **Ask an adult** to cut one piece open to check it is completely cooked through.

3 Meanwhile, make the dip. Mix the chilli powder with 15ml/1 tbsp of the water. **With adult supervision**, heat the oil in a small frying pan, and fry the onion and garlic until tender.

4 Turn down the heat and add the chilli paste and the remaining ingredients and stir. Stir in more water if the sauce is too thick and put it into a small bowl. Serve warm, with the chicken kebabs, cucumber slices and lemon wedges.

Super-duper Soup

Easy to make as there's no need to be too fussy – just chop up whichever vegetables you prefer and simmer them gently with tomatoes and stock. Serve with crusty bread.

SERVES 4–6
15ml/1 tbsp oil
1 onion, sliced
2 carrots, sliced
675g/1½lb potatoes, cut in
   large chunks
1.2 litres/2 pints/5 cups
   vegetable stock
450g/1lb can chopped tomatoes
115g/4oz broccoli, cut in florets
1 courgette (zucchini), sliced
115g/4oz mushrooms, sliced
7.5ml/1½ tsp medium-hot
   curry powder (optional)
5ml/1 tsp dried mixed herbs
salt and pepper

COOK'S TIP
This tasty soup freezes really well, so make double the amount and freeze half for another time. Then when you want it, simply defrost it in the refrigerator overnight or in a microwave and then heat it in a pan until it is piping hot.

1 Peel the onion, then cut it in half and slice it, **with adult supervision**. Peel the carrot and slice it into medium-thickness rounds.

2 With adult supervision, heat the oil in a large pan and fry the onion and carrots gently, until they start to soften.

3 Add the potatoes and fry gently for 2 minutes more, stirring often to prevent them from sticking. Add the stock, tomatoes, broccoli, courgette and mushrooms.

4 Add the curry powder (if using), herbs and salt and pepper and bring to the boil. Put the lid on and simmer for 30–40 minutes, or until tender. Taste and adjust the seasoning.

Cock-a-noodle Soup

Take a tasty trip to the Far East, with this Chinese-style soup.
It is packed with vibrant veggies such as corn and carrots.
You can try to use chopsticks to eat it!

SERVES 4–6
15ml/1 tbsp sesame oil
4 spring onions (scallions),
   roughly chopped
225g/8oz skinless chicken breast
   fillets, cut in small cubes
1.2 litres/2 pints/5 cups
   chicken stock
15ml/1 tbsp soy sauce
115g/4oz/1 cup frozen corn
115g/4oz medium thread
   egg-noodles
salt and pepper
1 carrot, thinly sliced
   lengthways, to garnish
prawn crackers, to serve
   (optional)

COOK'S TIPS
• You could use chunks of white
fish, king prawns (jumbo shrimp),
turkey, pork or whatever protein
you have to hand in place of the
chicken in this dish.
• For a vegetarian version, fry cubes
of tofu or some vegetable protein
instead of chicken, or just use
vegetables and noodles.

1 With adult supervision, heat the
oil and fry the spring onions and
chicken until the meat has browned
all over.

2 Add the stock and the soy sauce
and bring the soup to the boil.

3 Stir in the frozen corn (no need
to thaw it first), then add the
noodles, breaking them up roughly.
Taste the soup, and add salt and
pepper if needed.

4 Use small cutters to stamp out
shapes from the thin slices of carrot.
Add them to the soup. Simmer for
5 minutes, before serving in bowls
with prawn crackers, if you like.

See-in-the-dark Soup

Stop stumbling around when the lights are off – eat more carrots! Serve with crunchy toast.

SERVES 4

15ml/1 tbsp oil
1 onion, sliced
450g/1lb carrots, sliced
75g/3oz/½ cup split red lentils
1.2 litres/2 pints/5 cups
  vegetable stock
5ml/1 tsp ground coriander
75ml/3 tbsp chopped
  fresh parsley
salt and pepper

VARIATION

You could use a butternut squash instead of carrots for a change. **With adult supervision**, peel off the skin using a peeler (you may need help if the skin is very tough), then ask an adult to split the squash in half. Scoop out the seeds (roast them for a tasty snack) and cut the squash flesh into cubes.

1 With adult supervision, heat the oil and fry the onion until it is starting to brown. Add the sliced carrots and fry gently for 4–5 minutes, stirring them often, until they soften.

3 Add the lentils, stock and coriander to the pan with a little salt and pepper. Stir to combine then bring the soup to the boil.

COOK'S TIP

If you don't have a food processor or blender, push the soup through a strainer with a wooden spoon or leave it chunky.

2 Meanwhile, put the lentils in a bowl and cover with cold water. Remove any bits that float. Tip the lentils into a strainer and rinse under the cold tap.

4 Turn down the heat, put the lid on the pan and leave to simmer gently for 30 minutes, or until the lentils are cooked.

5 Add the chopped parsley and cook for 5 minutes more. Remove the soup from the heat and allow to cool slightly.

6 Carefully put the soup into a food processor or blender and whizz until it is smooth, **with adult supervision**. (You may have to do this half at a time.) Rinse the pan before pouring the soup back in and add a little water if it looks too thick. Heat up the soup again before serving it piping hot.

Tasty Toasts

Next time friends come over to watch a movie, surprise them with these delicious treats. Sweet peppers and oozy goat's cheese make a mouthwatering pairing.

SERVES 4
2 red (bell) peppers, halved
  lengthways and seeded
30ml/2 tbsp oil
1 garlic clove, peeled
  and crushed
1 French stick
45ml/3 tbsp pesto
50g/2oz/⅓ cup soft
  goat's cheese

VARIATIONS
• You can use lots of different toppings on these tasty toasts. Replace the (bell) peppers with sliced tomatoes and the goat's cheese with mozzarella for an Italian feast, and add olives, tuna or strips of ham to turn it into a more substantial snack.
• You could also use different bread, such as ciabatta or even crusty white bread instead of a French stick, if you prefer.

1 With adult supervision, put the pepper halves, cut-side down, under a hot grill (broiler) and let the skins blacken. Carefully put the halves in a plastic bag, tie the top and leave until cool enough to handle. Remove from the bag, peel off the skins and cut the peppers into strips.

2 Put the oil in a small bowl and stir in the crushed garlic. Cut the bread into slanting slices and brush one side with the garlic oil. Arrange the slices on a grill pan, and brown under a hot grill **with adult supervision**.

3 Turn the slices over carefully and brush the untoasted sides with the garlic oil and then spread evenly with the pesto using a palette knife or spatula.

4 Arrange pepper strips over each slice and put small wedges of goat's cheese on top. Put back under the grill and toast until the cheese has browned and melted slightly.

Spicy Cheese Nachos

Viva Mexico! Silence that hungry tummy with a truly spicy snack. Make it as cool or as hot as you like, by adjusting the amount of sliced jalapeño peppers. Olé!

SERVES 4
50g/2oz Cheddar cheese
50g/2oz Red Leicester cheese
50g/2oz pickled green
   jalapeño chillies
115g/4oz bag chilli
   tortilla chips

For the dip:
30ml/2 tbsp lemon juice
1 avocado, roughly chopped
1 beefsteak tomato,
   roughly chopped
salt and pepper

COOK'S TIP
• You can use some store-bought guacamole or tomato dip if you prefer, or why not try some sour cream and chive dip or hummus to ring the changes.
• You do not have to use chillies if you do not like spicy food.

1 Carefully grate the Cheddar chese and Red Leicester and slice the pickled jalapeños into rounds, **with adult supervision**.

2 Arrange the tortilla chips in an even layer on a flameproof plate that can be used under the grill (broiler). Sprinkle all the grated cheese over and then sprinkle as many jalapeños as you like over the top.

3 **With adult supervision**, place the plate under a hot grill and toast until the cheese has melted and browned – keep an eye on the chips to make sure they don't burn.

4 Mix the lemon juice, avocado and tomato together in a bowl. Add salt and pepper to taste and serve with the chips. Try scooping up some of the dip with the cheesy chips.

Wicked Tortilla Wedges

A tortilla is a thick omelette with lots of cooked potatoes in it. It is very popular in Spain, where it is cut in thick slices like a cake and served with bread. Try it with sliced tomato salad.

SERVES 4
30ml/2 tbsp oil
675g/1½lb potatoes,
    cut in small chunks
1 onion, sliced
115g/4oz mushrooms, sliced
115g/4oz/1 cup frozen
    peas, thawed
50g/2oz/⅓ cup frozen
    corn, thawed
4 eggs
150ml/¼ pint/⅔ cup milk
10ml/2 tsp Cajun seasoning
30ml/2 tbsp chopped
    fresh parsley
salt and pepper

1 With adult supervision, heat the oil in a large frying pan and fry the potatoes and onion for 3–4 minutes, stirring often. Turn down the heat, cover the pan and fry gently for another 8–10 minutes, until the potatoes are almost tender.

2 Add the mushrooms to the pan and cook for 2–3 minutes more, stirring often, until they have softened a little.

3 Add the peas and corn to the pan, and stir them into the potato mixture.

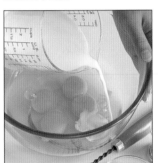

4 Put the eggs, milk and Cajun seasoning in a bowl. Add salt and pepper to taste and beat well.

5 Pat the vegetables so they are in an even layer and sprinkle the parsley on top. Pour the egg mixture over and cook over a low heat for 10–15 minutes.

6 Ask an adult to put the pan under a hot grill (broiler) to set the top of the tortilla. Serve hot or cold, cut into wedges.

COOK'S TIPS
• Use less Cajun seasoning if you do not like spicy food.
• Make sure the frying pan can be used under the grill (broiler).

Give 'Em A Roasting

Don't stick to roast spuds! A good roasting brings out the tastes and textures of other vegetables too.

SERVES 4

1 aubergine (eggplant), cut in large chunks
15ml/1 tbsp salt
1 red (bell) pepper, seeded and cut in thick strips
1 green (bell) pepper, seeded and cut in thick strips
1 yellow (bell) pepper, seeded and cut in thick strips
1 courgette (zucchini), cut in large chunks
1 onion, cut in thick slices
115g/4oz small mushrooms
225g/8oz plum tomatoes, quartered
75ml/5 tbsp olive oil
4–5 thyme sprigs
2 oregano sprigs
3–4 rosemary sprigs
salt and pepper

1 Arrange the aubergine chunks on a plate and sprinkle them with the salt. Leave for about 30 minutes for the salt to draw out the moisture.

2 Squeeze the aubergine to remove as much liquid as possible. Rinse off the salt. This process stops the aubergine tasting so bitter.

3 Preheat the oven to 200°C/400°F/Gas 6. Arrange all the vegetables, including the aubergine, in a roasting pan and drizzle the oil over.

4 Sprinkle most of the herb sprigs among the vegetables and season well. **Ask an adult** to put the pan into the hot oven and cook for 20–25 minutes.

5 Turn the vegetables over **with adult supervision** and cook them for 15 minutes more, or until they are tender and browned.

6 Sprinkle the remaining fresh herb sprigs over the cooked vegetables just before serving.

Chunky Veggie Salad

Something to really sink your teeth into – this yummy salad is choc-a-bloc with vitamins and energy. Serve on large slices of crusty bread for a filling meal.

SERVES 4

¼ small white cabbage
¼ small red cabbage
8 baby carrots, thinly sliced
50g/2oz small mushrooms, quartered
115g/4oz cauliflower, cut in small florets
1 small courgette (zucchini), grated
10cm/4in piece cucumber, cubed
2 tomatoes, roughly chopped
50g/2oz sprouted seeds
50g/2oz/½ cup salted peanuts
30ml/2 tbsp sunflower oil
15ml/1 tbsp lemon juice
salt and pepper
50g/2oz cheese, grated

COOK'S TIP

This super salad is really good for you as well as being very tasty. Try packing some in an airtight container and having it for lunch instead of sandwiches.

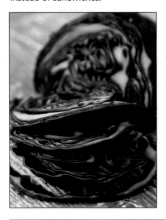

1 With adult supervision, finely chop the white and red cabbage.

2 Put all the prepared vegetables and the sprouted seeds in a large bowl and mix together well. Stir in the peanuts.

3 Drizzle the oil and lemon juice over. Season well and leave to stand for 30 minutes to allow the taste to develop.

4 Sprinkle grated cheese over just before serving on large slices of crusty bread. Have extra dressing ready, in case anybody wants more.

Yellow Chicken

An all-time Chinese classic that you can stir-fry in a few minutes. Yellow bean sauce is available in Chinese stores or large supermarkets. Serve with plain boiled rice.

SERVES 4
4 spring onions (scallions)
30ml/2 tbsp oil
75g/3oz/¾ cup salted
  cashew nuts
450g/1lb skinless chicken
  breast fillets, cut in strips
165g/5½oz jar yellow
  bean sauce

VARIATIONS
• You can add lots of vegetables to this stir-fry if you like. Sliced mushrooms, strips of (bell) pepper, carrot, celery and courgette (zucchini) all work really well – use whatever you like and is in the refrigerator.
• You could also use strips of steak or turkey fillet for a change.

COOK'S TIP
Cashew nuts are quite expensive, but you can buy broken cashews, which are cheaper and perfectly good for this dish. You could also use almonds, if you prefer.

1 With adult supervision, roughly chop the spring onions into small pieces using a sharp knife.

2 With adult supervision, heat 15ml/1 tbsp of the oil in a frying pan and fry the cashew nuts until browned. This does not take long, so keep an eye on them. Lift them out with a slotted spoon and put them to one side.

3 Heat the remaining oil and fry the spring onions and chicken for 5–8 minutes, until the meat is browned all over and cooked.

4 Return the nuts to the pan and pour the jar of sauce over. Stir well and cook gently until the mixture is hot. Serve immediately.

Pepperoni Pasta

Add extra zip to bland and boring pasta dishes with spicy pepperoni sausage. Quick and very tasty!

SERVES 4
275g/10oz/2½ cups dried pasta
175g/6oz pepperoni sausage, sliced
1 small or ½ large red onion, sliced
45ml/3 tbsp green pesto
150ml/¼ pint/⅔ cup double (heavy) cream
225g/8oz cherry tomatoes, halved
15g/½oz fresh chives
salt

VARIATIONS
• Use a mixture of red and yellow cherry tomatoes for a really cheerful meal.
• Serve with sesame bread sticks.

1 With adult supervision, peel the onion, cut it in half, trim off the base and top and then slice it across into half-moon shapes.

2 With adult supervision, cook the dried pasta in a large pan of lightly salted, boiling water, following the instructions on the packet.

3 Meanwhile, gently fry the pepperoni sausage slices and the onion together in a frying pan until the onion is soft. The oil from the sausage will mean you won't need extra oil.

4 Mix the pesto sauce and cream together in a small bowl. Add this cream mixture to the frying pan and stir until the sauce is smooth.

5 Add the cherry tomatoes and, **with adult supervision**, snip the chives over the top with scissors. Stir again.

6 Ask an adult to drain the pasta and tip it back into the pan. Pour the sauce over and mix well, making sure all the pasta is coated. Serve immediately.

Pancake Parcels

Be adventurous with your pancakes! Don't just stick to lemon and sugar: try this non-sweet version for a real change.

SERVES 4

For the pancakes:
115g/4oz/1 cup plain
    (all-purpose) flour
1 egg
300ml/½ pint/1¼ cups milk
2.5ml/½ tsp salt
25g/1oz/2 tbsp butter,
    for frying

For the filling:
200g/7oz/scant 1 cup cream
    cheese with chives
90ml/6 tbsp double
    (heavy) cream
115g/4oz ham, cut in strips
115g/4oz cheese, grated
15g/½oz/¼ cup fresh
    white breadcrumbs
salt and pepper

VARIATIONS
• You can use ready-made pancakes if you are in a hurry.
• You could swap the ham for strips of cooked chicken, drained canned tuna or cooked prawns (shrimp).

1 To make the pancakes, put the flour, egg, a little milk and the salt in a bowl and beat together with a wooden spoon to make a smooth paste. Gradually beat in the rest of the milk a little at a time, until the batter looks like thick cream. (The milk must be added slowly or the batter will be lumpy.)

2 **With adult supervision,** melt a little butter in a medium frying pan and pour in just enough batter to cover the base in a thin layer. Tilt and turn the pan to spread the batter out. Cook gently until set, then turn over with a spatula and cook the second side. If you feel brave, try tossing the pancakes!

3 Slide the pancake out of the pan. Make more pancakes in the same way – there should be enough batter to make four large ones. Stack in a pile, with a piece of greaseproof (waxed) paper between each one to stop them sticking to each other. Preheat the oven to 190°C/375°F/Gas 5.

4 Make the filling. Beat the cream cheese and cream in a bowl until it is smooth. Add the strips of ham and half the grated cheese, then season well with salt and pepper. Put a spoonful of the mixture in the middle of a pancake.

5 Fold one side over the mixture and then the other. Fold both ends up as well to make a small parcel. Arrange the parcels on a baking sheet, with the joins underneath. Make three more parcels in the same way.

6 Sprinkle the remaining cheese and the breadcrumbs over the parcels and cover them with foil. Cook for 20 minutes. **Ask an adult** to remove the foil. Cook for 10 minutes more, until browned. Tie green spring onion around the parcels, if you like.

Eggs in a Blanket

A hearty brunch or lunch to tuck into on a chilly day, with chunks of bread on the side.

SERVES 4

1 aubergine (eggplant), sliced
5ml/1 tsp salt
15ml/1 tbsp oil
1 onion, sliced
1 garlic clove, crushed
1 yellow (bell) pepper,
  seeded and sliced
1 courgette (zucchini), sliced
400g/14oz can chopped
  tomatoes
120ml/4fl oz/½ cup water
10ml/2 tsp dried mixed herbs
4 eggs
salt and pepper

COOK'S TIP

You could make the vegetable base of this scrummy dish the day before you need it, and store it in the refrigerator. Then all you need to do is put it back in a frying pan, heat it up and cook the eggs as described in step 4.

1 Arrange the aubergine slices on a plate, sprinkle with salt and leave for 30 minutes. Rinse and squeeze out as much juice as you can.

2 **With adult supervision**, heat the oil in a large frying pan. Fry the onion until it starts to soften. Add the garlic, pepper, courgette and aubergine and fry for 3–4 minutes.

3 Add the chopped tomatoes, water and herbs. Stir in salt and pepper to taste. Simmer gently for 5 minutes.

4 Make four shallow dips in the mixture and break an egg into each one. Cover the pan with a lid or foil and simmer for 8–12 minutes, until the eggs are set and the vegetables are tender.

Chicken Crisp

Forget all that spud-bashing – for a crunchy finish, top your pie with a packet of lightly salted crisps instead.

SERVES 4
115g/4oz/1 cup dried
   pasta shapes
175g/6oz broccoli,
   cut in florets
50g/2oz/¼ cup butter
1 red onion, thinly sliced
4 streaky (fatty) bacon rashers
   (strips), chopped
225g/8oz skinless chicken breast
   fillets, cut in chunks
60ml/4 tbsp plain
   (all-purpose) flour
450ml/¾ pint/scant 2 cups milk
salt and pepper

For the topping:
3 small packets of salted crisps
   (US potato chips)
75g/3oz cheese, grated

VARIATION
You could top the pie with mashed
potato if you prefer.

1 With adult supervision, cook the pasta in lightly salted, boiling water for 5 minutes. Add the broccoli and cook for 5 minutes more, until the pasta and broccoli are tender. **Ask an adult** to drain it well.

2 Meanwhile, **with adult supervision**, melt the butter in a pan and fry the onion until it starts to soften. Add the bacon and chicken and fry gently until browned all over. Add the flour and mix well.

3 Remove from the heat and gradually mix in the milk. Season, return to the heat and bring to the boil, stirring all the time. Stir in the pasta and broccoli. Preheat the grill (broiler).

4 Tip the mixture into a dish that can go under a grill. Cover the top with the crisps and sprinkle with the cheese. **Ask an adult** to put it under the grill for a few minutes, until the cheese has melted and browned.

Something Very Fishy

If you like getting your hands messy, this is the recipe for you! Serve with green vegetables and new potatoes.

SERVES 4

450g/1lb old potatoes, cut in small chunks
25g/1oz/2 tbsp butter
15ml/1 tbsp milk
412g/14½oz can pink salmon, drained, skinned and boned
1 egg, beaten
60ml/4 tbsp plain (all-purpose) flour
2 spring onions (scallions), finely chopped
4 sun-dried tomatoes in oil, chopped
grated rind of 1 lemon
oil, for frying
25g/1oz sesame seeds
salt and pepper

VARIATIONS

• You could swap the canned salmon for canned tuna, or flakes of fresh steamed fish if you prefer.
• You could also replace the fish with some grated cheese and roll the patties into log shapes.

1 With adult supervision, cook the potatoes in boiling salted water until tender. **Ask an adult** to drain them. Return to the pan. Add the butter and milk and mash until smooth. Season.

2 Put the mashed potato in a large bowl and beat in the salmon. Add the egg, flour, chopped spring onions, tomatoes and lemon rind. Mix well.

3 Divide the mixture into eight equal pieces and pat them into fish cake shapes, using floured hands as this helps to prevent the fish cakes from sticking.

4 Put the sesame seeds on a large plate and very gently press both sides of the fish cakes into them, until the cakes are lightly coated.

5 With adult supervision, pour oil into a frying pan to a depth of about 1cm/½in. Heat it gently. Put a small cube of bread in the pan and, if it sizzles, the oil is hot enough to cook the fish cakes. You will need to cook the fish cakes in several batches.

6 When one side is crisp and brown turn the cakes over carefully with a spatula and a fork, **with adult supervision**. The fish cakes are quite soft and need gentle treatment or they will break up. Lift them out and put them aside to drain on kitchen paper. Keep hot until they are all cooked, then serve.

Sticky Fingers

You have to like messy food to eat this popular dish,
so plenty of napkins please! Juicy tomatoes and fried
potatoes make the ideal accompaniment.

YOU WILL NEED
30ml/2 tbsp oil
1 onion, chopped
1 garlic clove, crushed
30ml/2 tbsp tomato
purée (paste)
15ml/1 tbsp white
wine vinegar
45ml/3 tbsp clear honey
5ml/1 tsp dried mixed herbs
2.5ml/¹/₂ tsp chilli powder
150ml/¹/₄ pint/²/₃ cup
chicken stock
8 chicken thighs
350g/12oz spare ribs
cherry tomatoes, to serve

For the potatoes:
675g/1¹/₂lb potatoes, cubed
30ml/2 tbsp oil
1 large onion, sliced
1 garlic clove, crushed
salt and pepper

1 With adult supervision, heat the oil in a pan and fry the onion and garlic for about 5 minutes, until the onion starts to soften.

2 Add the tomato purée, vinegar, honey, herbs, chilli powder and stock and bring to the boil. Lower the heat and simmer gently for 15–20 minutes, when the sauce should have thickened.

3 Preheat the oven to 190°C/375°F/ Gas 5. Arrange the chicken and ribs in a roasting pan.

4 Spoon the sauce evenly over the meat and cook for 30 minutes. **With adult supervision**, turn the meat over to ensure that it is coated evenly in the sauce.

5 Cook for 45 minutes more, turning the meat several times and spooning the sauce over. The meat should be really browned and sticky. Meanwhile, put the potatoes in lightly salted water, bring to the boil, then **ask an adult** to drain the poatoes well in a colander.

6 With adult supervision, heat the oil in a large frying pan. Fry the onion for about 10 minutes, until it starts to turn brown. Add the potatoes and garlic and fry for 25–30 minutes, until everything is cooked through, browned and crisp. Serve with the meat and tomatoes.

Tiny Toads

Serve these pint-sized portions of toad-in-the-hole with some lovely bright-green peas.

SERVES 4
115g/4oz/1 cup plain
  (all-purpose) flour
1 egg
300ml/½ pint/1¼ cups milk
45ml/3 tbsp fresh mixed herbs,
  e.g. parsley, thyme and chives,
  roughly chopped
24 cocktail sausages
salt and pepper

For the onion gravy:
15ml/1 tbsp oil
2 onions, sliced
600ml/1 pint/2½ cups stock
15ml/1 tbsp soy sauce
15ml/1 tbsp wholegrain mustard
30ml/2 tbsp cornflour (cornstarch)
30ml/2 tbsp water

COOK'S TIP
It is really important that the oil is sizzling hot when you add the batter to the pans, or they won't rise properly. **Ask an adult** to ladle it in as the oil may spit.

1 Preheat the oven to 200°C/400°F/ Gas 6. Put the flour, egg and a little milk in a bowl and mix well with a wooden spoon. Gradually mix in the rest of the milk to make a batter. Season well with salt and pepper and stir in the herbs.

2 Lightly oil eight 10cm/4in non-stick Yorkshire pudding tins (pans) and arrange three sausages in each. Cook in the hot oven for 10 minutes.

VARIATION
Use vegetarian sausages for friends who don't eat meat.

3 Ask an adult to take the tins out of the oven and use a ladle to pour batter into each tin. Put them back in the oven and cook for 30–40 minutes more, until the batter is risen and browned.

4 Meanwhile, **with adult supervision**, heat the oil in a pan. Fry the onions for 15 minutes until browned. Add the stock, soy and mustard and bring to the boil. Mix the cornflour and water together and pour into the gravy. Bring to the boil, stirring. Serve with the 'toads'.

Cherry Tomato Coca

This looks rather like a pizza but tastes very different.

SERVES 4

225g/8oz/2 cups strong white
  bread flour
5ml/1 tsp salt
6g/¼oz sachet easy-blend
  (rapid-rise) yeast
200ml/7fl oz/scant 1 cup
  hand-hot water
1 egg, beaten
45ml/3 tbsp poppy seeds
2 red (bell) peppers, seeded
  and cut in strips
1 red onion, cut in strips
225g/8oz cherry tomatoes,
  halved
45ml/3 tbsp olive oil
salt and pepper
fresh basil leaves, to garnish

COOK'S TIP

If you want to get ahead, you can
make the dough and knead it, but
instead of leaving it in a warm
place for 30–45 minutes, cover it
and place it in the refrigerator to
rise slowly overnight. Then you just
need to roll it out, add your
toppings and cook it as normal.

1 Put the flour, salt and yeast in
a bowl and mix well. Add half the
water and mix with a blunt knife.
Add the rest of the water and use
your hands to pull the mixture
together to make a dough.

2 Put the dough on a lightly floured
surface and knead for 5 minutes,
until it is no longer sticky but
smooth and stretchy. Put in a bowl,
cover with clear film (plastic wrap)
and leave for 30–45 minutes in a
warm place, until doubled in size.

3 Meanwhile, preheat the oven to
200°C/400°F/Gas 6. Knead the
dough again and roll or press it out
into a rectangular shape about
5mm/¼in thick. Place the dough on
a baking sheet. Brush the edges with
the beaten egg, then sprinkle the
edges with poppy seeds.

4 Sprinkle the prepared vegetables
on the unseeded central area and
drizzle the oil over the top. Sprinkle
with salt and pepper and cook for
30–40 minutes, until the dough has
risen and browned and the
vegetables have cooked. Garnish
with basil and serve hot or cold.

Raving Ravioli

Have a raving good time making your own pasta – get your
friends to help, then you can enjoy eating it together.

SERVES 4
75g/3oz fresh spinach, torn up,
  with tough stalks removed
275g/10oz/2½ cups strong
  white bread flour
3 eggs, beaten
15ml/1 tbsp oil
salt and pepper
300ml/½ pint/1¼ cups double
  (heavy) cream
15ml/1 tbsp chopped fresh
  coriander (cilantro)
30ml/2 tbsp grated Parmesan
  cheese, plus extra to serve

For the filling:
115g/4oz trout fillet, poached
  and drained, skin and
  bones removed
50g/2oz/⅓ cup ricotta cheese
grated rind of 1 lemon
30ml/1 tbsp chopped fresh
  coriander (cilantro)
salt and pepper

1 Steam the spinach over a pan of boiling water until it wilts, **with adult supervision**. Allow to cool, and squeeze out as much water as you can. Put it into a food processor, with the flour, eggs, oil and seasoning and whizz until it forms a dough.

2 Place the dough on a lightly floured surface and knead it for 5 minutes, until smooth. Wrap it in clear film (plastic wrap) and chill in the refrigerator for 30 minutes.

3 Sprinkle the work surface with flour. Roll out the dough to make a 50 x 46cm/20 x 18in shape, so the dough is the thickness of thin card. Leave to dry for 15 minutes. Use a sharp knife or pastry wheel to trim the edges and cut the dough in half.

4 Put the trout in a small bowl. Add the ricotta, lemon rind, coriander and salt and pepper and beat together. Put four spoonfuls of the filling across the top of the dough, leaving a small border round the edge. Carry on to make eight rows. Lift up the second sheet of pasta on a rolling pin and lay it over the first sheet.

5 Run your finger between the bumps to remove any air and to press the dough together. Using a knife or pastry wheel, cut the ravioli into small parcels and trim round the edge as well, to seal each one. **With adult supervision**, cook in salted boiling water for 8–10 minutes. Drain and return to the pan.

6 **With adult supervision**, put the cream, remaining coriander and the Parmesan in a pan and heat gently, without boiling. Pour over the ravioli and stir until evenly coated. Serve immediately, garnished with a sprig of coriander and Parmesan. Hand extra Parmesan round, if you like.

Homeburgers

These look the same as ordinary burgers, but watch out for the soft, cheesy middle. Serve with French fries and tomatoes.

SERVES 4

450g/1lb lean minced
 (ground) beef
2 slices of bread, crusts
 removed
1 egg
4 spring onions (scallions),
 roughly chopped
1 garlic clove, peeled
 and chopped
15ml/1 tbsp mango chutney
10ml/2 tsp dried mixed herbs
50g/2oz/⅓ cup mozzarella
 cheese
salt and pepper
4 burger buns, to serve

COOK'S TIPS

• These burgers can be frozen once
you have shaped them, while they
are still raw. Thaw them overnight
in the refrigerator before cooking
them as per the recipe.
• You could also pan-fry these
burgers. They will need about
5 minutes on each side, but cut
one open to check it is cooked.

1 Put the mince, bread, egg,
spring onions and garlic in a food
processor. Add a little salt and
pepper and, **with adult supervision**,
whizz until evenly blended. Add the
chutney and herbs and whizz again.

2 Divide the mixture into four
equal portions and pat flat, with
damp hands, to stop the meat
from sticking.

3 Cut the cheese into four equal
pieces and put one in the middle of
each flattened beef patty. Wrap the
meat round the cheese to make a
fat burger. Cover and chill in the
refrigerator for 30 minutes. **Ask
an adult** to preheat the grill
(broiler) to high.

4 **Ask an adult** to put the burgers
on a rack under the hot grill, but
not too close or they will burn on
the outside before the middle has
cooked properly. Cook them for
5–8 minutes on each side, then put
each burger in a roll, along with
your preferred trimmings.

Popeye's Pie

Tuck into this layered pie and you, too, can have bulging muscles like the cartoon character!

SERVES 4
75g/3oz/⅓ cup butter
5ml/1 tsp grated nutmeg
900g/2lb fresh spinach,
  washed and any large
  stalks removed
115g/4oz/⅔ cup feta
  cheese, crumbled
50g/2oz Cheddar cheese,
  grated
275g/10oz filo pastry sheets
10ml/2 tsp mixed ground
  cinnamon, nutmeg and
  black pepper

COOK'S TIPS
• It is important to really squeeze out as much liquid as possible from the spinach, or it will make the pastry soggy, which isn't very nice!
• Filo pastry dries out very quickly once it is exposed to air, so make sure you cover any that you are not using with a slightly damp dish cloth. It is also quite fragile, so try not to tear it as you lay it in the roasting pan.

1 With adult supervision, melt 25g/1oz/2 tbsp of the butter in a frying pan, add the nutmeg and the spinach and season. Cover and cook for 5 minutes. Drain well, pressing out as much liquid as possible.

2 Preheat the oven to 160°C/325°F/Gas 3. Melt the remaining butter in a pan. Mix the cheeses together and season them with salt and pepper. Unfold the pastry so the sheets are flat. Use one to line part of the base of a small, deep-sided, greased roasting pan. Brush with melted butter. Keep the remaining filo sheets covered with a damp tea towel.

3 Continue to lay pastry sheets across the base and up the sides of the pan, brushing each time with butter, until two-thirds of the pastry has been used, allowing the sheets to flop over the edges. Mix the cheeses and spinach together, and spread in the tin. Fold the pastry edges over.

4 Crumple up the remaining sheets of pastry and arrange them over the top. Brush with melted butter and sprinkle over the mixed spices. Cook for 45 minutes. Raise the oven temperature to 200°C/400°F/Gas 6, for 10–15 minutes more, to brown the top. Serve hot or cold.

Turkey Surprise Packages

This looks just like a paper parcel but there's a special treat inside. Put a parcel on each plate, with new potatoes and green vegetables, and let everyone open their own surprise.

SERVES 4

30ml/2 tbsp chopped parsley
4 turkey breast steaks, weighing
   150–175g/5–6oz each
8 streaky (fatty) bacon
   rashers (strips)
2 spring onions (scallions),
   cut in thin strips
50g/2oz fennel, cut in thin strips
1 carrot, cut in thin strips
1 small celery stick or a
   courgette (zucchini), cut in
   thin strips
grated rind and juice of 1 lemon
salt and pepper
lemon wedges, to serve

VARIATIONS

• Fennel tastes like aniseed or liquorice, so leave it out if you don't like that taste.
• You could use asparagus or baby corn instead of, or as well as the fennel.

1 Pat parsley over each turkey breast steak, then wrap two rashers of bacon round each one.

2 Preheat the oven to 190°C/375°F/ Gas 5. Cut four 30cm/12 in circles out of baking parchment or greaseproof (waxed) paper and put a turkey breast just off middle on each one.

3 Arrange the vegetable strips on top of the steaks, sprinkle the lemon rind and juice over and season well with salt and pepper.

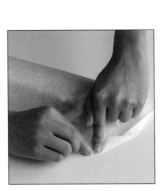

4 Fold the paper over the meat and vegetables and, starting at one side, twist and fold the paper edges together securely.

5 Work your way round the semi-circle, to seal the edges of the parcel together neatly.

6 Put all four parcels in a roasting pan and cook for 35–45 minutes, or until the meat is cooked and tender. **Ask an adult** to help you check that the steaks are cooked right through. Serve the packages sealed, so that diners can open them themselves, with lemon wedges to squeeze over.

Fish 'n' Rice

This tasty paella-type meal uses a frozen fish and shellfish
mixture that saves lots of preparation time.

SERVES 4
30ml/2 tbsp oil
1 onion, sliced
1 red (bell) pepper, seeded
  and chopped
115g/4oz mushrooms, chopped
10ml/2 tsp ground turmeric
225g/8oz/scant 1½ cups rice
  and grain mix (or rice)
750ml/1¼ pints/3 cups stock,
  made with a pilau-rice
  stock (bouillon) cube
400g/14oz bag frozen
  premium fish and shellfish
  selection, thawed
115g/4oz frozen large tiger
  prawns (shrimp), thawed
salt and pepper

VARIATION
If you don't like this fish mixture,
choose your own – use more
prawns (shrimp) and crab sticks if
you prefer, but cut down on the
fish cooking time.

1 With adult superivision, cut the
pepper in half, remove the seeds
and chop them into pieces. Wipe
the mushrooms with a piece of
damp kitchen paper to clean them,
if necessary, then slice.

2 Ask an adult to heat the oil in a
deep frying pan and fry the onion
for about 5 minutes, until it is
starting to soften. Add the chopped
pepper and mushrooms and fry for
1 minute

3 Stir in the turmeric and then the
grains. Stir until well mixed, then
carefully pour on the stock. Season
with salt and pepper, cover with a
lid or foil and leave to simmer
gently for 15 minutes.

4 With adult supervision, add the
fish and shellfish selection and
the prawns, stir well and turn up the
heat slightly to bring the liquid back
to the boil. Cover again and simmer
for 15–20 minutes more, until the
grains are cooked and the fish is
hot. Serve immediately.

Honey Chops

These tasty sticky chops are very quick and easy to prepare and grill, but they would be just as good cooked on a barbecue. Serve with herby mashed potatoes or fries.

SERVES 4
450g/1lb carrots
15ml/1 tbsp butter
15ml/1 tbsp soft brown sugar
15ml/1 tbsp sesame seeds

For the chops:
4 pork loin chops
50g/2oz/¼ cup butter
30ml/2 tbsp clear honey
15ml/1 tbsp tomato
  purée (paste)

COOK'S TIPS
• If the chops are very thick, put them under a medium-hot grill (broiler) and cook for longer to make sure the chops are cooked in the middle.
• This honey paste would also be delicious spread on juicy ribs or sausages, which can then be grilled (broiled) in the same way.

1 Cut the carrots into matchstick shapes, put them in a pan and just cover them with cold water. Add the butter and brown sugar and, **with adult supervision**, bring to the boil. Turn down the heat and leave to simmer for 15–20 minutes, until most of the liquid has boiled away.

2 Line the grill (broiler) pan with foil and arrange the pork chops on the grill rack. Beat the butter and honey together and gradually beat in the tomato purée, to make a smooth paste. Preheat the grill to high.

3 Spread half the honey paste over the chops and, **with adult supervision**, grill (broil) them for about 5 minutes, until browned.

4 **Ask an adult** to turn the chops over, spread them with the remaining honey paste and return to the grill. Grill the second side for a further 5 minutes, or until the meat is cooked through. Sprinkle the sesame seeds over the carrots and serve with the chops.

Bo Peep's Treat

Racks of lamb are actually lamb chops, called 'best end', that are still joined together. Serve with minty peas.

SERVES 4
2 racks of lamb, with at least
 four chops in each piece
25g/1oz/2 tbsp butter
4 spring onions (scallions),
 roughly chopped
115g/4oz/⅔ cup basmati rice
300ml/½ pint/1¼ cups stock
1 large ripe mango, peeled and
 roughly chopped
salt and pepper

For the roast potatoes:
900g/2lb potatoes, peeled and
 cut in large, even pieces
30ml/2 tbsp oil
15ml/1 tbsp coarse sea salt

COOK'S TIP
Tell your butcher that you are
cooking a 'Guard of Honour' and
he will prepare the meat for you.

1 With adult supervision, use a sharp knife to cut the meat off the ends of the bones. Discard the thick, fatty skin and scrape the bones as clean as possible. Chop the trimmings into small pieces and save them for the stuffing. (The butcher can do all this, if you prefer.)

4 Remove from the heat, stir in the mango and taste the stuffing. Add salt and pepper. Preheat the oven to 190°C/375°F/Gas 5.

2 Interlock the bones of the two racks of lamb like fingers, and tie the two sides together with a piece of cook's string between each two chops. Stand the racks in a large roasting pan.

5 Put the stuffing in the middle of the chops. Wrap the ends of the bones in a thin strip of foil and put the roasting pan in the oven. Cook for 30 minutes.

3 With adult supervision, melt the butter in a pan, add the onions and lamb trimmings and fry until the meat has browned. Add the rice, stir and pour in the stock. Bring to the boil, lower the heat, put a lid on the pan and leave to simmer for 8–10 minutes, until the rice is tender.

6 While the meat is cooking, make deep cuts in the rounded side of each potato **with adult supervision**. Put them in a pan with cold, salted water. Bring to the boil. Drain and arrange round the outside of the meat. Drizzle the oil over, sprinkle with sea salt and return to the oven for 1–1½ hours, until the potatoes are crisp and the meat is cooked.

Chocolate Puffs

These are always very popular and are so easy, fun and cheap to make they are sure to become a family classic.

SERVES 4–6
150ml/¼ pint/⅔ cup water
50g/2oz/¼ cup butter
65g/2½oz/generous ½ cup
  plain (all-purpose) flour, sifted
2 eggs, beaten

For the filling and icing:
150ml/¼ pint/⅔ cup double
  (heavy) cream
225g/8oz/1½ cups icing
  (confectioners') sugar
15ml/1 tbsp unsweetened
  cocoa powder
30–60ml/2–4 tbsp water

COOK'S TIPS
• It is very important that you make a hole in the bottom of each puff to let the steam out or it will make the puffs all soggy.
• The puffs can be made in advance and stored in an airtight container once they are dry and cooled.

1 Put the water in a pan, add the butter and, **with adult supervision**, heat gently until it melts. Bring to the boil and remove from the heat. Tip in all the flour at once and beat quickly until the mixture sticks together, leaving the side of the pan clean. Leave to cool slightly.

2 Add the eggs, a little at a time, and beat each time, by hand with a wooden spoon or with an electric whisk, until the mixture is thick and glossy and drops reluctantly from a spoon (you may not need to use all of the egg). Preheat the oven to 220°C/425°F/Gas 7.

3 Dampen two baking sheets with cold water and put walnut-sized spoonfuls of the mixture on them. Leave some space for them to rise. Cook for 25–30 minutes, until they are golden brown and well risen. Use a spatula to lift them on to a wire rack and make a small hole in each one with the handle of a wooden spoon to allow the steam to escape. Leave to cool.

4 Make the filling and icing. Whip the cream until it is thick. Put it into a piping bag fitted with a plain or star nozzle. Push the nozzle into the hole in each puff and squirt a little cream inside. Put the icing sugar and cocoa in a small bowl and stir together. Add enough water to make a thick glossy icing. Spread a spoonful of icing on each puff and serve.

Let's Get Tropical

Supermarkets are full of weird and wonderful fruits that make a really tangy salad when mixed together. Serve this fruity medley with cream or yogurt.

SERVES 4
1 small pineapple
2 kiwi fruit
1 ripe mango
1 watermelon slice
2 peaches
2 bananas
60ml/4 tbsp tropical fruit juice

COOK'S TIPS
• This tropical fruit salad is packed with vitamins and minerals as well as being really tasty.
• You can make this salad a few hours in advance and store it in the refrigerator, but add the bananas at the last minute as they will go brown and soggy if you leave them for long.

1 With adult supervision, cut the pineapple into 1cm/½in slices. Work round the edge of each slice, cutting off the skin and any spiky bits. Cut each slice into wedges and put them in a bowl.

2 With adult supervision, use a potato peeler to remove the skin from the kiwi fruit. Cut them in half lengthways and then into wedges. Add to the fruit bowl.

3 With adult supervision, cut the mango lengthways into quarters and cut round the large flat stone (pit). Peel the flesh and cut it into chunks or slices.

4 With adult supervision, cut the watermelon into slices, cut off the skin and cut the flesh into chunks. Remove the seeds. Cut the peaches in half, remove the stones and cut the flesh into wedges. Slice the bananas. Add all the fruit to the bowl and gently stir in the fruit juice.

Monster Meringues

A mouthwatering dessert made from meringue, whipped cream and tangy summer fruits.

SERVES 4
3 egg whites
175g/6oz/³⁄₄ cup caster
  (superfine) sugar
15ml/1 tbsp cornflour
  (cornstarch)
5ml/1 tsp white wine vinegar
a few drops of vanilla extract
225g/8oz assorted red
  summer fruits
300ml/¹⁄₂ pint/1¹⁄₄ cups double
  (heavy) cream
1 passion fruit

COOK'S TIP
• Draw six 7.5cm/3in circles and
pipe smaller meringues, if you
aren't hungry enough for this
monster dessert.
• Eat the desserts immediately
once assembled.

1 Preheat the oven to 140°C/275°F/
Gas 1. In pencil, draw eight 10cm/
4in circles on two separate sheets
of baking parchment which will fit
on two flat baking sheets.

2 Put the egg whites into a very
clean, dry bowl and whisk until stiff.
This will take about 2 minutes with
an electric whisk; peaks made in the
meringue should keep their shape
when it's ready. Add the sugar
gradually and whisk well each time.
The mixture should now be very stiff.

3 Use a metal spoon to gently stir
in the cornflour, white wine vinegar
and vanilla extract. Put the
meringue into a large piping bag,
fitted with a large star nozzle.

4 Pipe a solid layer of meringue in
four of the circles and then pipe a
lattice pattern in the other four. **Ask
an adult** to put the meringues in the
oven. Cook for 1¹⁄₄–1¹⁄₂ hours, **asking
an adult** to swap the shelf positions
after 30 minutes, until they are
lightly browned.

5 **With adult supervision**, roughly
chop most of the summer fruits,
reserving a few for decoration. Whip
the cream and spread a layer over the
solid meringue shapes.

6 Sprinkle the fruit over the top of
the cream. Halve the passion fruit,
scoop out the seeds with a
teaspoon and sprinkle them over
the chopped fruit. Put a lattice lid
on top of each of the desserts and
serve immediately with the reserved
fruits on the side.

Lazy Pastry Pudding

You don't need to be neat to make this dessert as it looks best when it's really craggy and rough. Serve with whipped cream or custard.

SERVES 6
225g/8oz/2 cups plain
  (all-purpose) flour
15ml/1 tbsp caster
  (superfine) sugar
15ml/1 tbsp ground mixed
  spice (apple pie spice)
150g/5oz/²/₃ cup butter
  or margarine
1 egg, separated
450g/1lb cooking apples
30ml/2 tbsp lemon juice
115g/4oz/²/₃ cup raisins
75g/3oz/½ cup demerara
  (raw) sugar
25g/1oz/¼ cup hazelnuts,
  toasted and chopped

COOK'S TIP
Try to be gentle with pastry and use just your fingertips to rub in the fat, as you can make it a bit tough if you handle it too much. Keep your hands cool by running them under cold water before touching the pastry.

1 Put the flour, sugar and spice in a bowl and stir. Add the butter or margarine and rub it into the flour with your fingertips, until the mixture looks like breadcrumbs. Add the egg yolk and use your hands to pull the mixture together. (You may need to add a little water.)

2 Turn on to a lightly floured surface and knead gently until smooth. Roll out the pastry to make a rough circle about 30cm/12in across. Use the rolling pin to lift the pastry on to a small baking sheet. The pastry should hang over the edges.

3 Peel and slice the apples **with adult supervision**. Toss them in the lemon juice, to stop them from turning brown. Sprinkle some of them over the middle of the pastry, leaving a 10cm/4in border all round. Sprinkle some of the raisins over the top. Reserve 30ml/2 tbsp of the demerara sugar, then sprinkle some of the remaining demerara sugar over. Keep making layers of apple, raisins and sugar until you have used them all up.

4 Preheat the oven to 200°C/400°F/ Gas 6. Fold up the pastry edges to cover the fruit, overlapping it where necessary. Don't worry too much about neatness. Brush the pastry with the egg white and sprinkle over the reserved demerara sugar. Sprinkle the nuts over the top. Cover the central hole with foil, to stop the raisins from burning. Cook for 30–35 minutes, until the pastry is cooked and browned. Leave to cool slightly before serving.

Life's a Peach!

A simple, rich dessert that's quick and easy to make. Serve it solo or with cream or yogurt.

SERVES 4
115g/4oz/1 cup raspberries
30ml/2 tbsp icing
    (confectioners') sugar
4 ripe peaches
120ml/8 tbsp mascarpone
45ml/3 tbsp soft brown sugar

COOK'S TIPS
• As the mascarpone melts, the sugar might slip off the fruit, so have some extra handy to sprinkle over the top of the peaches as soon as this happens.
• The raspberry sauce is also delicious served with raw peach slices and/or with yogurt or vanilla ice cream.
• Try to use nice ripe peaches. They should smell fragrant and be slightly soft to the touch but not have visible bruises or bad bits on the outside. If they seem dry when you cut them, you can moisten them by brushing over a little orange juice before you cook them under the grill (broiler).

1 Reserve a few of the raspberries for decoration and put the rest in a blender with the icing sugar and whizz until smooth, **with adult supervision**. Use a hand-held blender if you prefer, or push the raspberries through a strainer and then mix with the sugar.

2 Cut round each peach lengthways and twist the fruit. One half should come away, leaving the stone (pit) in the second half. Scoop the stone out with a teaspoon and arrange all eight peach halves on a grill (broiler) pan, cut-sides up. Preheat the grill.

3 Put 15ml/1 tbsp of cheese in the middle of each peach, in the dip left by the stone. Sprinkle the sugar over the top of all the peaches and, **with adult supervision**, grill (broil) under a medium heat, until the cheese and sugar have melted.

4 Share the raspberry sauce among four plates and arrange the peaches on top. Decorate with the reserved fruit and serve immediately.

Summer Fruit Cheesecake

Making this is much easier than it looks, and it tastes so good, it's well worth the extra effort.

SERVES 8–10

175g/6oz/³⁄₄ cup butter
225g/8oz digestive biscuits
   (graham crackers)
rind and juice of 2 lemons
11g/scant ½oz sachet gelatine
225g/8oz/1 cup cottage cheese
200g/7oz/scant 1 cup soft
   cream cheese, at room
   temperature
400g/14oz can condensed milk
450g/1lb/4 cups strawberries
115g/4oz/1 cup raspberries

COOK'S TIPS

• Always add gelatine to the liquid, never the other way round.
• Make sure the cream cheese is at room temperature before you process it or it may go grainy.

1 Grease and line the base of a 20cm/8in loose-bottomed springform cake tin (pan). **With adult supervision**, melt the butter in a pan over a low heat. Whizz the digestives in a food processor until they are crumbs. Stir into the butter.

2 Tip the biscuit crumb and butter mixture into the cake tin and use a spoon to spread the mixture in a thin, even layer over the base, pressing down well to compact it. Put the tin in the refrigerator while you make the filling.

3 Put the lemon rind and juice in a small bowl and sprinkle the gelatine over. Stand the bowl in a pan of water and, **with adult supervision**, heat gently, until the gelatine crystals have all melted. Stir the mixture and leave to cool slightly.

4 **With adult supervision**, put the cottage cheese in a food processor and whizz for 20 seconds. Add the cream cheese and condensed milk, fix the lid on again and whizz the mixture. Pour in the dissolved gelatine mixture and whizz again until everything is well combined.

5 **With adult supervision**, roughly chop half the strawberries, and arrange them over the biscuit base. Add half the raspberries. Pour the cheese mixture carefully over the fruit and level the top. Return to the refrigerator and leave overnight to set.

6 Carefully loosen the edges of the cheesecake with a spatula. Then stand the cake tin on a large mug or can and gently open the clip at the side of the tin. Allow the tin to slide down. Put the cheesecake on a serving plate and decorate it with the reserved fruit.

Chocolate Cups

Perfect for the chocoholics in the family. Serve with crisp dessert cookies.

SERVES 4
200g/7oz bar plain
  (semisweet) chocolate
120ml/4fl oz/½ cup double
  (heavy) cream
75g/3oz white chocolate

VARIATION
Try using white chocolate drops, chocolate-covered raisins or a chopped chocolate bar, instead of the white chocolate.

COOK'S TIP
It is very important that chocolate does not get too hot when it is melting as this will make it 'seize' and go grainy. Keep it away from the simmering water.

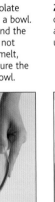

1 Break half the plain chocolate into pieces and put them in a bowl. **With adult supervision**, stand the bowl over a pan of hot, but not boiling, water and leave to melt, stirring occasionally. Make sure the water does not touch the bowl.

2 Line four ramekins or similar-sized cups with a piece of foil. Don't worry about the foil creasing or scrunching up – it doesn't matter.

3 Use a clean paintbrush or a pastry brush to spread the melted chocolate over the foil in a thick layer. Place in the refrigerator and leave until set. Paint a second layer of chocolate over the first and leave to set again.

4 Put the cream in a bowl and whisk until stiff with a balloon whisk or an electric whisk (**with adult supervision**). Melt the remaining plain chocolate as before and use a metal spoon to fold it into the cream.

5 **With adult supervision**, roughly chop the white chocolate and stir it gently into the chocolate and cream mixture.

6 Carefully peel the foil off the chocolate cups and fill each one with the chocolate and cream mixture. Chill in the refrigerator until set.

Ice Cream Bombes

This chilly dessert with warm sauce will have you ready to explode – it's dynamite!

SERVES 6
1 litre/1¾ pints/4 cups
   soft-scoop chocolate ice cream
475ml/16fl oz/2 cups
   soft-scoop vanilla ice cream
50g/2oz/⅓ cup plain (semisweet)
   chocolate drops
115g/4oz toffees
75ml/5 tbsp double
   (heavy) cream

VARIATIONS
• You could leave a small well in the vanilla ice cream layer and fill it with strawberry ice cream to create three-tiered bombes.
• For chocolate-toffee sauce, add a few squares of dark (bittersweet) chocolate to the melted toffees before you add the cream. The chocolate will melt in the heat from the dissolved toffees.

COOK'S TIP
You can store any sauce that doesn't get used in a container in the refrigerator for about 5 days.

1 Share the chocolate ice cream between six small cups. Push it roughly to the base and up the sides, leaving a small cup-shaped dip in the middle. Return to the freezer and leave for 45 minutes. Take it out again and smooth the ice cream into shape. Return to the freezer.

2 Put the vanilla ice cream in a small bowl and break it up slightly with a spoon. Stir in the chocolate drops and then use this mixture to fill the dip in the chocolate ice cream. Return the cups to the freezer and leave overnight.

3 Put the toffees in a small pan and, **with adult supervision**, heat gently, stirring all the time. As they melt, add the cream and keep mixing until all the toffees have melted and the sauce is warm.

4 Dip the cups in hot water and run a knife or spatula round the edge of the ice cream to separate it from the cup. Turn out on to individual plates and pour the toffee sauce over the top. Serve immediately.

Puffy Pears

An eye-catching dessert that is simple to make and delicious to eat, especially when served with whipped cream or crème fraîche.

SERVES 4
225g/8oz puff pastry
2 pears, peeled
2 squares plain (semisweet)
   chocolate, roughly chopped
15ml/1 tbsp lemon juice
1 egg, beaten
15ml/1 tbsp caster
   (superfine) sugar

VARIATIONS
• Try the same thing using eating apples, especially when you have picked the fruit yourself.
• Instead of placing chocolate in the cavities of the pears, you can use almond paste. Simply mix 30ml/2 tbsp ground almonds with enough lemon juice to make a stiff paste, then roll this into four small balls and put one in the hollow in each pear.
• For a lovely golden glaze, brush the top of the pastry with a little beaten egg before baking the pear puffs in the oven.

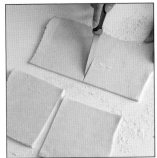

1 Roll the pastry into a 25cm/10in square on a lightly floured surface. **With adult supervision**, trim the edges, then cut it into four equal smaller squares.

2 With adult supervision, remove the core from each pear half and pack the gap with the chopped chocolate. Place a pear half, cut-side down, on each piece of pastry and brush them with the lemon juice, to prevent them from going brown.

3 Preheat the oven to 190°C/375°F/ Gas 5. Cut the pastry into a pear shape, by following the lines of the fruit, leaving a 2.5cm/1in border. Use the trimmings to make leaves and brush the pastry border with the beaten egg.

4 Arrange the pastry and pears on a baking sheet. **With adult supervision**, make deep cuts in the pears, taking care not to cut all the way through, and sprinkle them with the caster sugar. Cook for 20–25 minutes, until lightly browned. Serve hot or cold.

Chocolate Brownies

Scout out these delicious, moist and chewy cakes, and guide yourself to a chocolate treat!

MAKES 9

65g/2½oz/⅓ cup butter
50g/2oz plain (semisweet) chocolate
150g/5oz/scant 1 cup soft light brown sugar
2 eggs, beaten
65g/2½oz/generous ½ cup plain (all-purpose) flour
50g/2oz/½ cup roughly chopped pecans or walnuts
25g/1oz/¼ cup icing (confectioners') sugar

VARIATIONS

• You could leave out the nuts if you prefer.
• For a healthier brownie, use half plain (all-purpose) flour and half wholemeal (whole-wheat) flour.

1 Put the butter and chocolate in a bowl and stand it over a pan of hot, but not boiling water, **with adult supervision**. Make sure the water doesn't touch the bowl. Leave until they have both melted and then stir them together.

2 Stir the sugar into the butter and chocolate mixture and leave for a while to cool slightly.

3 Cut a piece of baking parchment or greaseproof (waxed) paper to fit the base of an 18cm/7in square cake tin (pan).

4 Preheat the oven to 180°C/350°F/Gas 4. Beat the eggs into the chocolate mixture, then stir in the flour and nuts, taking care not to over-mix – the mixture should be just combined.

5 Pour the mixture into the lined cake tin and level the top. Cook for 25–35 minutes, until firm around the edges but still slightly soft in the middle. Try not to overcook the brownies or they will be dry.

6 **With adult supervision**, cut into nine squares and leave to cool in the tin. Dredge the top with a little icing sugar and serve hot or cold.

Bacon Twists

Making bread is always fun, so try this unusual version and add a twist to your breakfast. Serve with soft cheese with herbs.

MAKES 12
450g/1lb/4 cups strong
  white bread flour
6g/¼oz sachet easy-blend
  (rapid-rise) yeast
2.5ml/½ tsp salt
400ml/14fl oz/1¾ cups
  hand-hot water
12 streaky (fatty) bacon
  rashers (strips)
1 egg, beaten

COOK'S TIP
This same basic dough mix can be used to make rolls or a loaf of bread. Rolls will take the same amount of time, but a loaf will take about 30 minutes. Tap the base of the bread – if it sounds hollow, it's cooked. If not, return it to the oven for 5 minutes more.

1 Mix the flour, yeast and salt in a bowl and stir them together. Add a little of the water and mix together with a blunt knife.

2 Add the remaining water a little at a time and use your hands to pull the mixture together, to make a sticky dough.

3 Turn the dough on to a lightly floured surface and knead it for 5 minutes, or until the dough is smooth and stretchy.

4 Divide into 12 pieces and roll each one into a sausage shape.

5 Lay each bacon rasher on a chopping board and, **with adult supervision**, run the back of the knife down its length, to stretch it slightly. Wind a rasher of bacon round each dough 'sausage'.

6 Brush the 'sausages' with beaten egg and arrange them on a lightly oiled baking sheet. Leave the sheet somewhere warm for 30 minutes, or until they have doubled in size. Preheat the oven to 200°C/400°F/Gas 6 and, **with adult supervision**, cook the 'sausages' for 20–25 minutes, until they cooked and browned. Cool on a wire rack.

Gingerbread Jungle

Snappy cookies in animal shapes, which can be decorated in your own style, so get creative!

MAKES 14
175g/6oz/1½ cups self-raising (self-rising) flour
2.5ml/½ tsp bicarbonate of soda (baking soda)
2.5ml/½ tsp ground cinnamon
10ml/2 tsp caster (superfine) sugar
50g/2oz/¼ cup butter
45ml/3oz/3 tbsp golden (light corn) syrup
oil, for baking sheets
50g/2oz/½ cup icing (confectioners') sugar
5–10ml/1–2 tsp water

COOK'S TIPS
• You can stamp out any shapes you like with this dough – stars, reindeer or snowmen for Christmas, rabbits for Easter, hearts for Valentine's day – the choice is only limited by what cutters you have!
• Little brothers and sisters may like to help stamp out and decorate these cookies.

1 Preheat the oven to 190°C/375°F/ Gas 5. Put the flour, bicarbonate of soda, cinnamon and sugar in a bowl and mix together. **With adult supervision**, melt the butter and syrup in a small pan. Pour over the dry ingredients.

2 Mix together well using a spoon and then use your hands to pull the mixture together to make a dough.

3 Turn the dough on to a lightly floured surface and roll it out to a thickness of about 5mm/¼in using a rolling pin.

4 Use animal cutters to cut shapes from the dough and arrange them on two lightly oiled baking sheets, leaving enough room between them to rise and spread a bit. Press the dough trimmings back into a ball, roll it out and cut more shapes. Continue to do this until all of the dough is used up.

5 **With adult supervision**, cook the cookies for 8–12 minutes, until they are lightly browned. Leave the cookies to cool slightly before lifting them on to a wire rack with a palette knife to cool completely. Meanwhile, sift the icing sugar into a small bowl and add enough water to make a fairly soft icing.

6 Put the icing in a piping bag fitted with a small, plain nozzle and pipe decorations on the cookies.

Blueberry Muffins

Monster muffins that contain whole fresh blueberries that burst in the mouth when bitten.

MAKES 9
375g/13oz/3¼ cups plain
  (all-purpose) flour
200g/7oz/scant 1 cup caster
  (superfine) sugar
25ml/1½ tbsp baking powder
175g/6oz/¾ cup butter,
  roughly chopped
1 egg, beaten
1 egg yolk
150ml/¼ pint/⅔ cup milk
grated rind of 1 lemon
175g/6oz/1½ cups fresh
  blueberries

VARIATION
You can use other fruits such as raspberries or blackberries in place of the blueberries if you like. It is best to use fresh berries rather than thawed frozen ones as these tend to be too wet and can make the muffin soggy.

1 Preheat the oven to 200°/400°F/ Gas 6. Line a muffin tin (pan) with nine large paper muffin cases.

3 In a separate small bowl, beat the egg, egg yolk, milk and lemon rind together with a fork.

COOK'S TIP
As the muffins have fresh fruit in them, they will not keep for longer than four days in an airtight container, so it is best to eat them immediately! You could also freeze some of them if you don't think they will be eaten before the fruit goes mouldy.

2 Put the flour, sugar, baking powder and butter in a bowl. Use your fingertips to rub the butter into the flour, until the mixture looks like breadcrumbs.

4 Pour the egg and milk mixture into the flour mixture, add the blueberries and mix gently together with a wooden spoon.

5 Divide the mixture among the cake cases and cook for 30–40 minutes, until they are risen and brown on top.

6 **With adult supervision**, push a skewer into the middle of one of the muffins. The muffins are cooked if it comes out clean. Lift on to a wire rack to cool.

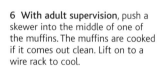

Chunky Choc Bars

A no-cook cake that's a smash-hit with everyone.

MAKES 12

350g/12oz plain (semisweet)
  chocolate
115g/4oz/½ cup butter
400g/14oz can condensed milk
225g/8oz digestive biscuits
  (graham crackers), broken
50g/2oz/⅓ cup raisins
115g/4oz ready-to-eat dried
  peaches, roughly chopped
50g/2oz hazelnuts or pecans,
  roughly chopped

VARIATIONS

You can use any chopped dried
fruit in these delicious, rich bars.
Try dried cranberries, soft dried
mango or dried cherries. You can
also use different types of cookies,
such as ginger cookies, or choc-
chip cookies for an even more
intense chocolate hit!

1 Line an 18 x 28cm/7 x 11in cake
tin (pan) with some clear film
(plastic wrap).

2 **With adult supervision**, put the
chocolate and butter in a large bowl
over a pan of hot but not boiling
water (the bowl must not touch
the water) and leave to melt. Stir
until well mixed, then remove from
the heat.

3 Beat the condensed milk into the
chocolate and butter mixture with a
wooden spoon.

4 Add the cookies, raisins, peaches
and nuts and mix well, until all the
ingredients are coated in chocolate.

5 Tip the mixture into the prepared
tin, making sure it is pressed well
into the corners. Leave the top
craggy. Put in the refrigerator and
leave to set.

6 Lift the cake out of the tin using
the clear film and then peel it off.
Cut into 12 bars and keep chilled –
until you are ready to eat it!

Peanut Cookies

Packing up a picnic? Got a birthday party coming up?
Make sure some of these nutty cookies are on the menu.

MAKES 25

225g/8oz/1 cup butter
30ml/2 tbsp smooth
  peanut butter
115g/4oz/1 cup icing
  (confectioners') sugar
50g/2oz/scant ½ cup cornflour
  (cornstarch)
225g/8oz/2 cups plain
  (all-purpose) flour
115g/4oz/1 cup unsalted
  peanuts

COOK'S TIPS

• Make really monster cookies by
making bigger balls of dough. Leave
plenty of room on the baking
sheets for them to spread, though,
and they will take a little longer
to cook.
• Make sure you use unsalted, not
salted, peanuts!
• You can use crunchy peanut
butter if you prefer – whichever
you have in the kitchen is fine.

1 Put the butter and peanut butter
in a bowl and beat together. Add
the icing sugar, cornflour and plain
flour and mix together with your
hands, to make a soft dough

2 Preheat the oven to 180°C/350°F/
Gas 4 and lightly oil two baking
sheets. Roll the mixture into 25
small balls, using floured hands, and
place the balls on the two baking
sheets. Leave plenty of room for the
cookies to spread.

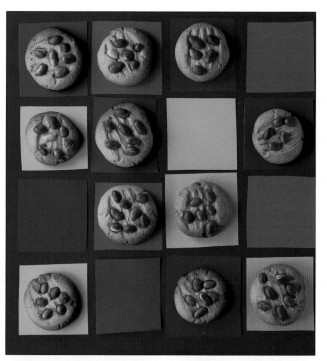

3 Press the tops of the balls of
dough flat, using either the back of
a fork or your fingertips, which you
should wet first to prevent them
from sticking to the dough.

4 Press some of the peanuts into
each of the cookies. **With adult
supervision**, cook for 15–20 minutes,
until lightly browned. Leave to cool
for a few minutes before lifting
them on to a wire rack with a
palette knife or spatula.

Five-spice Fingers

These light, crumbly cookies have an unusual Chinese five-spice taste that is just delicious.

MAKES 28
115g/4oz/½ cup butter
    or margarine
50g/2oz/½ cup icing
    (confectioners') sugar
115g/4oz/1 cup plain
    (all-purpose) flour
10ml/2 tsp five-spice powder
oil, for greasing
grated rind and juice of
    ½ orange

VARIATIONS
• You could pipe these cookies into round whirls, or just spoon them into small mounds, if you prefer.
• For a decadent finish, dip each end of the cookies into melted chocolate once they have cooled. You could even then sprinkle the melted chocolate with hundreds and thousands.
• If you don't have any five-spice, you could use 5ml/1 tsp vanilla extract instead.

1 Put the butter or margarine and half the icing sugar in a large bowl and beat with a wooden spoon, until the mixture is smooth, creamy and soft.

2 Add the flour and five-spice powder and beat again. Put the mixture in a large piping bag fitted with a large star nozzle. Preheat the oven to 180°C/350°F/ Gas 4.

COOK'S TIP
These cookies are delicious served with ice cream or creamy desserts such as mousse.

3 Grease two baking sheets and pipe short lines of mixture, about 7.5cm/3in long, on them. Leave enough room for them to spread. Cook for 15 minutes, until lightly browned. Leave to cool slightly, then lift them on to a wire rack.

4 Sift the remaining icing sugar into a small bowl and stir in the orange rind. Add enough juice to make a thin icing and brush it over the cookies while they are still slightly warm.

Carrot Cake

This tasty cake is really good for you, as well as being moist, soft and great to look at.

SERVES 10–12
225g/8oz/2 cups self-raising
  (self-rising) flour
10ml/2 tsp baking powder
150g/5oz/1 scant cup soft light
  brown sugar
115g/4oz ready-to-eat dried
  figs, roughly chopped
225g/8oz carrots, grated
2 small ripe bananas, mashed
2 eggs
150ml/¼ pint/⅔ cup sunflower
  or vegetable oil
175g/6oz/¾ cup cream cheese,
  at room temperature
175g/6oz/1½ cups icing
  (confectioners') sugar, sifted
small, bright sweets (candies),
  nuts or grated chocolate,
  to decorate

1 Lightly grease an 18cm/7in round, loose-based springform cake tin (pan). **With adult supervision**, cut a piece of baking parchment to fit the base of the tin.

2 Preheat the oven to 180°C/350°F/ Gas 4. Put the flour, baking powder and sugar into a large bowl and mix well using a wooden spoon. Stir in the figs.

3 Using your hands, squeeze as much liquid out of the grated carrots as you can and add them to the bowl containing the flour mixture. Mix in the mashed bananas.

4 Beat the eggs and oil together and pour them into the mixture. Beat together with a wooden spoon until well combined.

COOK'S TIP
Because this cake contains moist vegetables and fruit, it will not keep longer than a week, but you probably won't find this a problem!

5 Spoon the mixture into the prepared tin and level the top. Cook for 1–1¼ hours, until a skewer pushed into the middle of the cake comes out clean. **Ask an adult** to remove the cake from the tin and leave to cool on a wire rack.

6 Beat the cream cheese and icing sugar together, to make a thick icing. Spread it over the top of the cold cake. Decorate with small sweets, nuts or grated chocolate. Cut in small wedges, to serve.

Lemon Meringue Cakes

This is a delicious variation on fairy cakes – soft lemon sponge topped with crisp meringue.

MAKES 18

115g/4oz/½ cup butter or margarine
200g/7oz/scant 1 cup caster (superfine) sugar
2 eggs
115g/4oz/1 cup self-raising (self-rising) flour
5ml/1 tsp baking powder
grated rind of 2 lemons
30ml/2 tbsp lemon juice
2 egg whites

VARIATION

Use a mixture of oranges and lemons, for a sweeter taste.

1 Preheat the oven to 190°C/375°F/ Gas 5. Put the butter or margarine in a bowl and beat until soft. Add 115g/4oz/½ cup of the sugar and continue to beat until the mixture is smooth and creamy.

2 Beat in the eggs, flour, baking powder, half the lemon rind and all the lemon juice.

4 Whisk the egg whites in a clean bowl, until they stand in soft peaks.

3 Stand 18 small paper cases in two bun tins (pans), and share the mixture between them.

5 Stir in the remaining sugar and lemon rind.

6 Put a spoonful of the meringue mixture on each cake. Cook for 20–25 minutes, until the meringue is crisp and brown. Serve the cakes hot or cold.

COOK'S TIP

Make sure that you whisk the egg whites enough before adding the sugar – when you lift out the whisk they should stand in peaks that just flop over slightly at the top.

Citrus Punch and Spicy Nuts

This is a knock-out of a cold drink that goes down well on really hot days, served with spicy nuts.

SERVES 4

For the citrus punch:
juice of 2 pink grapefruit
juice of 2 lemons
juice of 4 oranges
150ml/¼ pint/⅔ cup
  pineapple juice
30ml/2 tbsp caster
  (superfine) sugar
600ml/1 pint/2½ cups
  lemonade
slices of lime and orange,
  to decorate

For the spicy nuts:
75g/3oz/⅓ cup butter
15ml/1 tbsp oil
2 garlic cloves, crushed
30ml/2 tbsp Worcestershire
  sauce
5ml/1 tsp chilli powder
5ml/1 tsp ground turmeric
5ml/1 tsp cayenne pepper
450g/1lb/4 cups mixed nuts

1 To make the citrus punch, put the fruit juices in a large jug (pitcher) or bowl, stir in the sugar, then chill.

2 Add the lemonade and fruit slices, just before serving.

3 Make the nuts while the punch is chilling. **With adult supervision**, heat the butter and oil in a frying pan until the butter melts. Stir in the garlic, Worcestershire sauce, spices and seasonings.

4 Cook gently for 1 minute, stirring all the time, then add the nuts and cook for 4-5 minutes, until lightly browned. Drain on kitchen paper and leave to cool before serving with the punch.

Buck's Fizzy and Twizzles

*Impress the grown-ups with your own corker of a drink,
which will knock spots off the real thing. Serve with tasty
cheese twizzles.*

SERVES 6–8

For the Buck's fizzy:
600ml/1 pint/2½ cups fresh
   orange juice
45ml/3 tbsp lemon juice
50g/2oz/½ cup icing
   (confectioners') sugar, sifted
300ml/½ pint/1¼ cups bitter
   lemon, chilled
orange slices, to decorate

For the twizzles:
225g/8oz/2 cups plain
   (all-purpose) flour
115g/4oz/½ cup butter,
   roughly chopped
15ml/1 tbsp dried mixed herbs
50g/2oz mature (sharp) Cheddar
   cheese, grated
cold water, to mix
salt and pepper

VARIATION
You could use lemonade in place of
the bitter lemon, if you prefer.

1 To make the Buck's fizzy, mix the
orange and lemon juice and the
icing sugar in a large jug (pitcher),
then chill.

2 Just before serving, add the bitter
lemon, stir to mix well and then
decorate the jug or the glasses with
orange slices.

COOK'S TIP
Make some of the pastry strips into
circles. After baking, slip three
pastry strips inside each circle so
each guest gets his or her personal
set of twizzles.

3 To make the twizzles, preheat the
oven to 190°C/375°F/Gas 5. Put the
flour and the butter in a bowl. Rub in
the butter, then stir in the herbs,
grated cheese and seasoning, and
add enough water to bring the pastry
together. Knead it into a firm dough.

4 Roll out the dough until it is 5mm/
¼in thick and cut it into 15cm/6in
strips, about 1cm/½in wide. Twist
each strip and arrange on a greased
baking sheet. Cook for 15–20 minutes,
until golden. **With adult supervision**,
transfer to a wire rack to cool.

Hot Chocolate and Choc-tipped Cookies

Get those cold hands wrapped round a steaming hot drink, and tuck into choc-tipped cookies.

SERVES 2 (THE DRINK)

For the hot chocolate:
90ml/6 tbsp drinking chocolate powder, plus a little extra for sprinkling
30ml/2 tbsp sugar, or more according to taste
600ml/1 pint/2½ cups milk
2 large squirts aerosol cream (optional)

For the choc-tipped cookies:
115g/4oz/½ cup soft butter or margarine
45ml/3 tbsp icing (confectioners') sugar, sifted
150g/5oz/1¼ cups plain (all-purpose) flour
a few drops of vanilla extract
75g/3oz plain (semisweet) chocolate

1 To make the drinking chocolate, put the drinking chocolate powder and the sugar in a pan. **With adult supervision**, add the milk and bring it to the boil, whisking all the time. Divide between two mugs. Add more sugar if needed. Top with a squirt of cream, if you like.

2 To make the choc-tipped cookies, put the butter or margarine and icing sugar in a bowl and beat them together until very soft. Mix in the flour and vanilla extract. Preheat the oven to 180°C/350°F/Gas Mark 4 and lightly grease two baking sheets with a little butter.

3 Put the mixture in a large piping bag fitted with a large star nozzle and pipe 10–13cm/4–5in lines on the baking sheets. Cook for 15–20 minutes, until pale golden brown. Allow to cool slightly before lifting on to a wire rack. Leave the cookies to cool completely.

4 Put the chocolate in a small bowl. **With adult supervision**, stand the bowl in a pan of hot, but not boiling, water and leave to melt. Dip both ends of each cookie in the chocolate, put back on the rack and leave to set.

COOK'S TIPS
Make round cookies if you prefer, and dip half of each cookie in melted chocolate.

Fruit Crush and Fruit Kebabs

Fruit crush is just the ticket on a sultry summer's day, served with mouthwatering fruit kebabs.

SERVES 6

For the fruit crush:
300ml/½ pint/1¼ cups
　orange juice
300ml/½ pint/1¼ cups
　pineapple juice
300ml/½ pint/1¼ cups tropical
　fruit juice
475ml/16fl oz/2 cups lemonade
fresh pineapple slices and fresh
　cherries, to decorate

For the fruit kebabs:
24 small strawberries
24 green seedless grapes
12 marshmallows
1 kiwi fruit, peeled and cut
　in 12 wedges
1 banana
15ml/1 tbsp lemon juice

1 To make the fruit crush, put the orange juice and the pineapple juice into ice-cube trays and freeze them until solid.

2 Mix together the tropical fruit juice and lemonade in a large jug (pitcher). Put a mixture of the ice cubes in each glass and pour the crush over. Decorate the glasses with the pineapple slices and cherries.

3 To make the fruit kebabs, carefully thread 2 strawberries, 2 grapes, a marshmallow and a wedge of kiwi fruit on to each of 12 wooden skewers. Take care as the skewers are sharp.

4 Peel the banana and cut it into 12 slices. Toss them in the lemon juice to stop them from going brown and thread on to the skewers. Serve the kebabs immediately.

COOK'S TIPS
You could use all sorts of other fruits to make these kebabs, such as chunks of mango, pineapple, or some blueberries.

Strawberry Smoothie and Stars-in-your-Eyes Cookies

A real smoothie that's lip-smackingly special, when served with crunchy stars-in-your-eyes cookies.

SERVES 4–6
For the strawberry smoothie:
225g/8oz/2 cups strawberries
150ml/¼ pint/⅔ cup Greek
  (US strained plain) yogurt
475ml/16fl oz/2 cups
  ice-cold milk
30ml/2 tbsp icing
  (confectioners') sugar

For stars-in-your-eyes cookies:
115g/4oz/½ cup butter
175g/6oz/1½ cups plain
  (all-purpose) flour
50g/2oz/¼ cup caster
  (superfine) sugar
30ml/2 tbsp golden
  (light corn) syrup
30ml/2 tbsp preserving sugar

VARIATIONS
• You can stamp out the cookies in any shape you like.
• Decorate the tops of the cookies with icing rather than sugar.

1 First make the stars-in-your-eyes cookies: put the butter, flour and sugar in a bowl and rub in the fat with your fingertips, until the mixture looks like breadcrumbs. Stir in the sugar and then knead together to make a ball. Chill in the refrigerator for 30 minutes.

2 Preheat the oven to 180°C/350°F/ Gas 4 and lightly grease two baking sheets with a little butter. Roll out the dough on a lightly floured surface to a thickness of about 5mm/¼in and use a 7.5cm/3in star-shaped cookie cutter to stamp out the cookies.

3 Arrange the cookies on a baking sheet, leaving enough room for them to rise and spread. Press the trimmings together and keep rolling out and cutting more cookies until all the mixture has been used. Bake for 10–15 minutes, until they are golden brown.

4 Put the syrup in a bowl and heat it on HIGH for 12 seconds, **with adult supervision**. Brush over the warm cookies. Sprinkle preserving sugar on top of each. Leave to cool.

5 To make the smoothies, reserve a few of the strawberries for decoration and put the rest in a blender with the yogurt. Whizz until fairly smooth, **with adult supervision**.

6 Add the milk and icing sugar to the food processor, process again and pour into glasses. Serve each glass decorated with one or two of the reserved strawberries.

INDEX